D0959774

HAIKU MIND

Haiku Mind

108 Poems to Cultivate Awareness and Open Your Heart

PATRICIA DONEGAN

Shambhala

BOSTON & LONDON · 2008

Shambhala Publications, Inc.
Horticultural Hall
300 Massachusetts Avenue
Boston, Massachusetts 02115
www.shambhala.com

9 8 7 6 5 4 3 2

Printed in the United States of America

⊛ This edition is printed on acid-free paper that meets the American National Standards Institute Z39.48 Standard.
♻ This book was printed on 30% postconsumer recycled paper. For more information please visit www.shambhala.com.
Distributed in the United States by Random House, Inc., and in Canada by Random House of Canada Ltd

Library of Congress Cataloging-in-Publication Data
Haiku mind: 108 poems to cultivate awareness and open your heart/[edited by] Patricia Donegan.—1st ed.
p. cm.
Includes bibliographical references and index.
ISBN 978-1-59030-579-9 (alk. paper)
1. Haiku, American. 2. Haiku—Translations into English. I. Donegan, Patricia.
PS593.H3H356 2008
808.81'41—dc22
2008015374

In gratitude, to my father and mother,
Daniel Patrick Donegan and Janet Caroline Donegan

CONTENTS

ACKNOWLEDGMENTS

Gratitude to many:

First, to Peter Turner, Shambhala's president, who believed in the vision of my book from the very beginning. And to the founder of Shambhala Publications, Sam Bercholz, who encouraged me to publish with Shambhala years ago. And to Hazel Bercholz who was the contact for this book and who comissioned the beautiful cover design reflecting the haiku moment.

To my editor at Shambhala, Jennifer Brown, whose patience and understanding kept me going and whose clear eyes helped shape the book. And to the other Shambhala editors, particularly Ben Gleason and Chloe Foster, who were kind with their "razor-sharp" pens.

To Yoshie Ishibashi, dearest friend and insightful researcher, whose help on the Japanese haiku translations and biographies was invaluable.

To Susan Edwards, a close friend and writer-metaphysician, who read parts of the manuscript and always gave her deep ideas and caring support.

To haiku poet and scholar William J. Higginson and to

secretary Lane Parker of the Haiku Society of America, for their help in contacting other haiku poets.

To my haiku teachers Seshi Yamaguchi and Kazuo Sato, to other haiku translators, and to the fine haiku poets who all gave me much inspiration.

To family and friends who were encouraging: especially my cousins Joan and Fred Anderson (Fred, in particular, with his "writer's eyes"); my cousins Judy and Dale Swafford; my lifetime friends Carter Eckert, Cheryl Hoiseth, Brigid Meier, Phyllis Anderson Meyer, Jean Westby, and Marianne Yamaguchi; and my aunt Eleanor Finkler also; but most of all, my mother and father who were kindly there for the birth of each of the 108 pieces.

To my brother Craig Donegan, a Tibetan Buddhist, who auspiciously gave me my first copy of a book by Chögyam Trungpa Rinpoche back in 1973.

To my meditation teachers, living and nonliving, especially Chögyam Trungpa Rinpoche (1939–1987) who helped me expand my vision, making this book possible.

INTRODUCTION

Cutting a pear
sweet drops drip
from the knife

SHIKI MASAOKA

I wanted to write this book to share the idea of "haiku mind"—a simple yet profound way of seeing our everyday world and living our lives with the awareness of the moment expressed in haiku—and to therefore hopefully inspire others to live with more clarity, compassion, and peace. The root of haiku mind is found in the widely-known poetic form of haiku, a form of poetry that contains seventeen syllables in three phrases (5-7-5) in Japanese or usually three lines in English. A fine haiku presents a crystalline moment of heightened awareness in simple imagery, traditionally using a *kigo* or season word from nature. It is this crystalline moment that is most appealing. However, this moment is more than a reflection of our day-to-day life—it is a deep reminder for us to pause and to be present to the details of the everyday. It is this way of being in the world with awakened open-hearted awareness—of being mindful of the ordinary moments of our lives—that I've come to call "haiku mind." My understanding of this view of haiku mind came out of my personal journey, and three profound teachings or awakenings.

It began with "seeing an orange"—it could have been a pear, but in my case it was an orange—in sunlight on the kitchen table. It was 1974 and I was living in Hawaii after my Peace Corps stint in Korea. I had just finished a one-week group meditation retreat with my first Zen meditation teacher, Robert Aitken Roshi, who often used haiku in his talks. I had come home tired and hungry and as I sat down to take my first spoonful of soup, I stopped in mid-air as I saw the orange in afternoon sunlight by my plate. The light was golden and the orange perfectly round. All was perfect as it was, and I felt suddenly and totally at peace as I saw "the thing itself" as it was in its nakedness without my overlay of thoughts or opinions, and tears rolled down my face. I had seen the orange clearly, as if for the first time—that was my first experience of haiku mind. The next week the Roshi told me that my experience was a tiny glimpse into awakened mind—which takes a lifetime or lifetimes of practicing meditation or practicing being aware, in order to deepen and incorporate into one's everyday life. As Basho, the greatest haiku master, said, "To learn about the pine tree you must become one with the pine and drop your self-centered view." It was only a glimpse, but it was an opening.

My second experience was "being put on the spot" by my main meditation teacher, the late Tibetan master

Chögyam Trungpa Rinpoche who founded Naropa University. Although he was not Japanese, he greatly appreciated the traditional arts of *ikebana, kyudo,* and haiku. It was 1980 and I had been teaching East-West poetics (including haiku) at Naropa under poet Allen Ginsberg for several years and was involved with Rinpoche's teaching of "dharma poetics": that any poetry can be a vehicle of awakening if done mindfully. It was here that my poetry and my meditation practice began to merge through haiku; I began to use haiku, not just as a literary form, but also as an awareness practice. This was due to Trungpa Rinpoche's ruthless kindness: at the three-month-long meditation retreat with several hundred people, I was "put on the spot." At the end of one of Rinpoche's talks late one night, without warning, he called me up in front of the large audience and asked me to compose a spontaneous poem, a haiku on the three kinds of Buddhism. I was handed the microphone. I was stunned: my mind was blank yet inspired. I was naked and immersed in the moment and simply recorded in words what was there in all of its nakedness. I looked at the shrine next to me and said, "between the altar candles the purple irises' shadows" as the first line; the second line came from staring at the hushed audience, "you look into my eyes, I look into yours," and then feeling my heart pounding, the concluding line, "only the empty heartbeats of the guru and us." It wasn't a perfect haiku or perhaps not even a haiku, but it was a perfect teaching for trusting my own haiku mind—of being totally open to the present moment, to what is there. And I felt grateful. I was put on the spot for five nights, but the first night was the real leap into seeing haiku as an awareness practice of the moment.

My third experience was "finding ordinary mind" in Japan. It was 1986 and I went to Japan to study with the late haiku master Seishi Yamaguchi—I initially had the romantic notion to find a Zen-like haiku master, but auspiciously I found a Robert Frost–like haiku master instead. It was in his weekly group class, where we all presented our haiku for correction by the teacher, that I learned how subtle and ordinary haiku really was—and that because it is so ordinary it seems extraordinary. In our discussions about haiku, the teacher and the other Japanese poets were puzzled why I even mentioned the subject of Zen, because for them haiku was about ordinary life: just that, nothing special, that there is absolutely no separation between the mundane and the sacred, things as they are. I then realized that to search for the so-called Zen mystery in every haiku is a mistake and to do so takes away the depth of their personal flavor and ordinary mind context. At that same time I also discovered Chiyo-ni—an eighteenth-century, woman haiku master and Buddhist nun—who was known to have lived *haikai no michi* (following the Way of Haiku in daily life) as espoused by Basho; she always used haiku as an *aisatsu* (greeting) to others and to the world of Nature in her everyday life by staying open to the present moment. As I began co-translating her haiku, I saw in her the real possibility of a way of seeing and being in the world—of daily living with this haiku mind, even with our busy lives today.

Over twenty years have passed, yet I am still on this journey. Just last year on my walks by Lake Michigan near my home, where I can feel the vastness of the lake and sky, I realized something further about haiku mind. Haiku mind is the awareness to tune in to the vastness of the moment. Actually to create and appreciate this tiny form of poetry, one needs a vast mind like the sky. This is known in Tibetan Buddhism as *dzogchen*: that our natural state of mind is vast and clear as the sky. When we can pause and relax in the moment, that is our haiku mind: the awakened, openhearted awareness that we can always tap into. Every good haiku captures such a moment and is a reflection of our haiku mind. Here haiku mind includes both mind and heart in a non-dualistic whole, as in the Chinese character for "mind-heart" where there is no separation. And when we are present, we can then see and appreciate the juicy pear or orange on the sunlit windowsill before we pick it up to eat it.

However, as we all know, these uncertain times of our present world call us to go beyond the awareness of just the pear, and to become more conscious and engaged in our world—we can do this by using this awareness of haiku mind as a stepping stone and expand it. We do this by simply practicing to pause in the moment. One way is pausing when we read the haiku in this book—for each haiku is a reminder of our innate haiku mind and is a powerful seed that grows into deeper awareness. This in turn leads to more pausing in our daily life when we slow down and take in a few breaths, which allows a small opening to occur, allows us to relax and see things beyond judgment of good or bad, things as they are in their nakedness: the pear in sunlight. For when we can relax our mind, we can feel a sense of open heartedness and peace—and even though small, it will grow little by little like a seed and will naturally give rise to extending out to others and to the world, beyond our self-concern. In this way, haiku and the root of haiku—our natural haiku mind—become a way to plant seeds of peace in our selves and in the world.

* * *

This is not just an anthology of haiku poems, but rather spiritual reflections on 108 haiku—I used 108 because it is an auspicious number in Buddhist thought as there are 108 difficulties to overcome in order to become awakened, and so there are 108 beads on a Buddhist *mala*. The reflective form I used was inspired by the Japanese tradition of the *haibun*: *hai* (haiku) and *bun* (sentences) combined; usually the story or reflection behind the poem. These reflections are meditations rather than literary analysis. Each of the 108 haiku is a meditative springboard for the contemplation of a specific theme, be it adversity, nowness, or compassion. My reflections are often in a poetic-prose style that are interwoven into a tapestry, using the thematic threads of the poetic, the spiritual, and the political. Hopefully each haiku and each reflection will encourage further contemplation—and will cultivate a sense of awareness, compassion, and peace.

Except for those poets who lived long ago, I've been fortunate over the years to have personally met or known the majority of these gifted poets included in this collection. Choosing the featured haiku was the challenge: matching good haiku to good themes for reflection. There were so many fine haiku poets whose work I wanted to include but couldn't, not just because of space limitations, but because I was not able to make the right match between the fine haiku and the theme for a reflection.

Above all, I have tried to represent a balance of poets: traditional and modern, Japanese and non-Japanese, male and female. Some haiku were my favorites, some by the famous, some by the less known, some by devoted haiku poets, some by those who seldom write or wrote haiku. Of the Japanese selections, I did not include any living poets because I am not as familiar with their work and there are so many fine traditional haiku poets who have rarely or never been presented in English. All the English translations from the

Japanese were done in collaboration with Yoshie Ishibashi; I hope they reflect some of their original haiku spirit.

Of the non-Japanese selections, I included mostly American haiku poets and some Canadians; I only wish that I could have been more knowledgeable to include more international haiku—the few non-English haiku included are my translated versions. Overall, each of the 108 haiku that was chosen embodies a clear presentation of the moment of now, which is always present when we pause. These haiku inspired me to pause and reflect and I hope they will inspire others as well.

This collection is intended for any reader, of whatever background, religion, or spiritual inclination, for the reflections, although greatly inspired by the Buddhist tradition, are taken from many "wisdom traditions." This collection is intended for any reader, whether interested in haiku or not. Above all, it is intended for any reader who is interested in cultivating awareness and opening the heart. The power of haiku is its ability to plant these seeds within us, to reawaken our haiku mind this very moment, as we gaze upon the pear and the world beyond it.

I originally envisioned this book to be written on a meditative retreat like Thoreau's *Walden*; however, it was written in snatches of respite in between caring for my parents; hopefully these circumstances deepened my view. In addition, several books of spiritual reflections transmitted a spark for this book, including *Comfortable with Uncertainty: 108 Teachings on Cultivating Fearlessness and Compassion* by Pema Chödrön and *The Hundred Verses of Advice* by Dilgo Khysentse Rinpoche. If there is any drop of insight in my reflections, it is due to the kindness of my teachers, Buddhist and otherwise, that I have been fortunate to meet, in this lifetime and perhaps others; may this work only be of benefit.

HAIKU MIND

pausing
halfway up the stair—
white chrysanthemums

ELIZABETH SEARLE LAMB

Pausing is the doorway to awakening. This haiku epitomizes a moment that occurs naturally in our lives, but that we often hurry or gloss over. Haiku awareness is a simple way to slow down and tune in to this fleeting moment, to appreciate what is right in front of us. We pause not only with our body but also with our mind. And sometimes we can be attentive and sometimes we cannot, but that is all right, for the next moment always brings us the fresh possibility to pause and be present again. There are no steps to follow, there is no enlightenment to work toward—there is only the simplicity of relaxing into this very moment that is complete in itself. This naked moment is the only guide that we need to relax our mind. We need to trust this: in the midst of our daily life activities, the possibility to slow down, to stop, and then to appreciate naturally unfolds. For a fleeting moment we pause and note the sunlight on the sheets as we make the bed, note the warm sun on our cup as we sip tea, or note the fading light on the curtain as we enter the room. And we let out a breath or sigh. Pausing.

ELIZABETH SEARLE LAMB (1917–2004). The foremost American haiku poet living a life dedicated to haiku, called "the first lady of American haiku." Lamb was one of the founding members in 1968, along with Harold G. Henderson, of the Haiku Society of America and editor of *Frogpond,* its journal. She was also an early president of HSA and an honorary curator of the American Haiku Archives. Her last book was *Across the Windharp: Collected and New Haiku.*

To see Void vast infinite
look out the window
into the blue sky.

ALLEN GINSBERG

This is Allen Ginsberg's death haiku, written about a week before he died. It is in the Japanese tradition of haiku poets and Zen masters to write "death poems," ideally as a way to keep one's awareness, even if sick and dying, in order to write last words that reflect one's understanding of life. As a practitioner of both meditation and haiku, Ginsberg told me on several occasions how much he admired this tradition and hoped he could do it someday. This "haiku" was actually one of his experimental forms of haiku called "American sentences," originally written in one line.

This haiku is a wonderful reminder of a simple practice in the Tibetan Buddhist tradition called *sky meditation:* looking up into the vast sky and feeling the large expanse of space, which stops our mind's preoccupation of the moment. The sky is merely a reminder of this openness that is always within us, that we can tap into anytime. Wherever we are, we can always simply stop and look up at the sky, or even imagine the sky . . . and breathe out a long-awaited sigh. For a moment we are back to our natural state of mind, which is as vast and open as the sky; all else is just thoughts and feelings like clouds passing by. In any moment we can come back to sky mind.

ALLEN GINSBERG (1926–1997). An American Beat outrider, one of the greatest visionary poets of the twentieth century. Allen was famous for his long political protest poems, beginning with *Howl* in 1955, yet he was also a lifelong practitioner of haiku as an "awareness practice," which fit in with his Buddhist meditation practice. For a selection of his haiku see the chapbook *Mostly Sitting Haiku* or his *Collected Poems 1947–1980;* for a selection of his experimental haiku called "American Sentences," see his last book, *Death and Fame: Last Poems 1993–1997.*

I kill an ant ...
and realize my three children
were watching

SHUSON KATO

The microcosm of one ant crawling across the floor and
our response to it. "Be honest to yourself; and write what
is there." These words are from the Japanese woman haiku
master, Teijo Nakamura, given in a rare interview when I had
asked her what was the greatest principle of haiku. At first
I thought the interpreter had made a mistake, for her reply
seemed much too simple; later when I tried to practice it, I
realized how hard yet truly profound it was. This haiku re-
flects the courage it takes to be that honest with oneself in
order to become a true human being who lives mindfully
moment to moment. As we all know, not causing harm to
oneself or others is the basis for creating more peace in our

own lives and those around us, extending out to the rest of the world. But it can only happen if we are honest and start where we are now, for honesty is the root of this transformation. Starting this very moment with whatever is happening and seeing it clearly with a gentle heart, no matter how embarrassing, how painful, how sad, no matter what: this is the human journey.

SHUSON KATO (1905–1993). One of the great modern Japanese haiku poets, Kato was also a Basho scholar. In the 1930s he was associated with the Ashibi school of poetry and their magazine, founded by Shuoshi Mizuhara, which emphasized a humanist perspective. Later in the 1940s he founded the *Kanrai* (Thunder in Midwinter) journal, and a collection of his haiku uses the same title.

don't hit the fly—
he prays with his hands
and with his feet

ISSA KOBAYASHI

The Dalai Lama was once asked how to teach children compassion in a world full of violence and intolerance. And he replied, "teach them to like and respect insects." For if we can learn to care about something that is tiny, strange, and not always easy to relate to, then we can realize that insects, like everything in Nature, share the same life. And in turn we could eventually realize that all human beings—not just our particular group or country—also share the same life. Haiku is a way to remember how everything is connected in our world, and if we feel connected we will not harm things, but rather care for them. Haiku is often about noticing and caring for the small; more than any other haiku poet, Issa was known for his compassion toward small creatures. This was an idea taken from Issa's belief in Pure Land Buddhism, namely that we should not harm any creatures, from human beings down to insects, and that we should have compassion toward them because we are all part of the same life force. Haiku is an apt reminder that in order to nurture our compassion toward other people and the world, we can begin by extending our compassion to all living things in Nature, by starting with insects like the tiny fly. Starting with the small.

ISSA KOBAYASHI (1763–1828). One of the three greatest traditional Japanese male haiku poets, along with Basho and Buson. As a Pure Land Buddhist, he espoused compassion for all living things, perhaps because he himself had a life of poverty and personal tragedy. See his autobiographical haibun collection, *Oraga Haru* (The Spring of My Life) from 1819.

summer grasses—
all that remains
of warriors' dreams

BASHO MATSUO

War: this haiku expresses its universal truth and could just have been written today as in ancient times. This was written in the seventeenth century as part of Basho's haibun (travel poems) when he was visiting an ancient samurai battlefield of the Fujiwara clan. It reflects his bereft feeling about the human condition; in fact, he said he wept as he looked out over the ruins. This haiku is a deep reflection on the truth of reality, which is by nature transient and fleeting. When we are unable to accept this truth we become distressed. However, recognition of this truth could at least bring a sense of poignancy to all of us human beings, who inevitably experience and witness it. There is even an aesthetic of this recognition

9

in Japan called *mono no aware* (the poignancy of transient things). And some meditation masters, such as the Vajrayana Buddhist teacher Chögyam Trungpa Rinpoche, have said that if we could expand our vision and really understand the naked truth of impermanence, we would be enlightened on the spot. Haiku could be helpful in this regard, for it is able to capture the moment of transience and hold it up to us like a mirror. We are the warriors, we are the dreams, we are the grasses: we are transient.

BASHO MATSUO (1644–1694). The greatest haiku poet in Japanese history. Coming from a low samurai class, he later became a renga master with many disciples, studied Zen, and traveled widely. He took haiku to a deeper level, espousing haikai no michi (the Way of Haiku) as a way of life and a return to Nature. See *Sarumino* (*Monkey's Raincoat*, a renga collection); and *Oku no Hosomichi* (*Narrow Road to the Interior*, a haibun collection). See also haiku translations in R. H. Blyth's *History of Haiku*, vol. 1 and Makoto Ueda's translation *Basho and His Interpreters*—just some among many translations.

rouged lips
forgotten—
clear spring water

CHIYO-NI

For a brief moment she forgot herself. This is one of Chiyo-ni's most memorable realization haiku. It shows her forgetting her rouged lips—the makeup that was important to women of her time and to women still today—while drinking the fresh water. This haiku epitomizes her unique style, combining clarity and sensuality, but most importantly it expresses the heightened awareness that comes when we forget the self and are present to the moment. If her mind had been worried, preoccupied with her makeup, she would not have been able to really see and appreciate the clear spring water from the flowing mountain stream, nor fully enjoy sipping it from her cupped hands. In that moment it was only, "ah! the clear spring water." In the words of Dogen, the thirteenth-century Zen master, "when we forget the self, we can remember the 10,000 things."[1] It is often hard but rewarding to switch our attention away from our self and notice the other, whether it be the tired face of a homeless person on the street corner or the luminous raindrops against the windowpane. Even to practice this a few minutes a day not only expands our awareness, but more important, it reminds us of our true humanity.

CHIYO-NI (1703–1775), or Kaga no Chiyo; her family name was Fukumasuya. One of the greatest traditional Japanese women haiku poets. Born into a scroll maker's family, she studied with two of Basho's disciples, was a renowned renga master, painter, and Buddhist nun. She published two poetry books: *Chiyo-ni Kushu* (Chiyo-ni's Haiku Collection) and *Matsu no Koe* (Voice of the Pine). Known for living Basho's "Way of Haiku." See *Chiyo-ni: Woman Haiku Master* by Patricia Donegan and Yoshie Ishibashi.

> violets here and there
> in the ruins
> of my burnt house

SHOKYU-NI

This haiku has haunted me: the poet's response to her personal tragedy and her original preface to this poem are inspirational, "On my return from Tsukushi at the close of March, I found that my hut had been destroyed by fire. Looking at the ruins, I composed this verse."[2] This haiku addresses the age-old question we all face: how to work with adversity, in our own lives and in this chaotic, imperfect world around us. We cannot ultimately control what happens, but we can control our response to what happens. This becomes the spiritual path for each of us, however we find it. We could cry and rage or deny what happens, which may be part of the process, and perhaps the process the poet went through herself before or after she wrote this haiku. Yet sometimes adversity can be an opportunity rather than an obstacle, if we are simply aware of our daily response to things, examine what happens with courage and openness, and possibly reflect upon it as in this haiku. It is not being optimistic or looking for a silver lining, but just seeing the way things are: the burnt charcoal of the wooden house and the tiny flowers growing nearby—to see the paradox, the complexity, how the good and bad are often intertwined. This haiku reminds us how to work with personal tragedy, how to work with natural disasters, plague, famine, and war—how to see violets in the ruins . . . or whatever happens to be there.

SHOKYU-NI (1713–1781); her family name was Yagi. One of the well-known Japanese women haiku poets of the Edo period (1603–1868). A renga master who studied with the poet Yaha, who was a close disciple of Basho. After her husband died she became a Buddhist nun, made a pilgrimage, and created her main work, *Kohaku-an-shu* (White Lake Hermitage Collection).

As my anger ebbs,
The spring stars grow bright again
And the wind returns.

RICHARD WRIGHT

Unknown to most people the famous novelist Richard Wright used haiku as a comforting awareness practice to get him through his declining health due to amebic dysentery complications the last year and a half of his life. He left a legacy of over four thousand haiku—amazingly, he hadn't written any haiku before then. Written in Paris cafés, written when bedridden, they helped him, as his daughter noted, "to spin these poems of light out of the gathering darkness."[3] In the 1950s, when meditating wasn't as popular as it is now, Wright found a way to work with the dark emotions of his anger and depression, in the ups and downs of his illness, which we all face in ourselves or others sometime or another.

The writing of haiku, which includes focusing on Nature, helps one do just that: get outside oneself and appreciate what is there. This haiku clearly records how his perception of Nature was clouded by his emotions, and that Nature did not change, but his perception changed when he became mindful and could see clearly again: the stars, the wind, what was there beside him all along.

RICHARD WRIGHT (1908–1960). An esteemed African-American novelist, born in rural Mississippi and died an expatriate in Paris. Wright was an early spokesperson for black Americans; with his novel *Native Son* (1940), he became a major literary voice; other works include *The Outsider, Black Boy,* and *Black Power.* Haiku, taken up in illness the last months of his life, written in traditional seventeen syllables, reflects his relationship to Nature with a universality unlike his other works. See *Haiku: This Other World* (1998).

remembering those gone
thankful to be here—
pond of purple iris

MARGARET CHULA

Gratitude: the word embodies a sacred worldview that is not only transformative but necessary in a world yearning for peace. In a way, this haiku itself embodies a threefold contemplation that we could easily follow as a prayerful reminder any time of the day, perhaps when we first arise or go to bed. Even in the midst of grief for the loss of loved ones, we can remember them gratefully: perhaps a parent, child, or spouse, our ancestral spirits, or those who died recently in a war zone. Remembering them is recognizing our inseparability and our deep connection; we know that without them we would not be here in the same way at all. With the thought of those gone, at the same time an appreciation for being here arises—just to be alive and breathing here and now (although not always perfectly), just to simply sit in a chair and feel our back against the wood is enough. It is at this point with an expansive, relaxed feeling of gratitude that we can then see and take in the vast world around us—the pond of purple iris. The beauty of this haiku is that it is really a simple prayer: gratitude for others, self, and the world of Nature—and beyond.

MARGARET CHULA (b. 1947). One of the foremost American haiku poets, distinguished by awards in haiku as well as related forms of haibun and tanka poetry, in addition to short stories. Chula lived in Kyoto, Japan, for twelve years, which deeply influenced her poetic sensibilities and international haiku activities. Her main works include *Grinding My Ink*, *Shadow Lines*, *The Smell of Rust*, and *What Remains: Japanese Americans in Internment Camps* with quilt artist Cathy Erickson.

bush warbler—
I rest my hands
in the wooden sink

CHIGETSU-NI

The bird called me out. I wanted to stay asleep under the covers, but the bird called me out. I was lost in a depressed thought and then the bird called me out. An unknown bird from an unknown tree called me out. We've all had this experience of being caught in our comfortable, habitual thoughts about this or that—and then something happens—there is a gap, a crack of space long enough for the sound of a bird to penetrate us, and we are awakened. This is sometimes referred to as a heightened moment of awakening, but actually it is an ordinary occurrence, yet feels extraordinary when we finally tune in to the present moment in all of its vividness. Here the poet found herself awakened from her everyday kitchen chores, if only for a brief interval, by the magical and subtle sound of a warbler. There is also the story of Ikkyu, the infamous Zen master–poet of the fifteenth century, who is said to have reached total enlightenment in his twenties while meditating in a boat on Lake Biwa, when hearing the caw, caw, cawing of a crow. The possibility to let the bird call us out, or to let something else call us out, is always there.

CHIGETSU-NI (1632–1708); her family name was Kawai. She was the closest woman disciple and friend of Basho, and one of the greatest traditional Japanese women haiku poets. After her husband died she became a Buddhist nun and lived in Otsu with her brother (and adopted son) Otokuni, a fine poet and also a student of Basho. She was one of the main contributors, along with Basho, to the famed *Sarumino* (*Monkey's Raincoat*) linked-verse collection.

> this world of dew
> is yes, a world of dew
> and yet . . .

ISSA KOBAYASHI

Sorrow beyond words. In every language the word *sorrow* embodies the same human emotion in all human beings, in all places, in all times—past, present, and future—on this earth. Feelings beyond words—described here by the poet Issa from his own personal tragedy. This is his most famous haiku, supposedly written after his one-year-old daughter Sato died of smallpox in 1818, as recorded in his haibun diary. Over his lifetime he experienced the infancy death of five of his children; besides this, he experienced the death of two wives, and also the burning-down of his house. This poem resonates because it is so real: this haiku was written for all of us who inevitably experience grief in our lives, as part of the human condition, of just being alive, of just dying, of just having a broken heart. He knows it is all as transient as "dew," and we know it is all transient as "dew," too, "and yet . . . ," he says. And when we think about it, or don't even think about it, something deep within us, within the human spirit, almost imperceptibly wants and needs to also say, whether in a shout or whisper, "and yet . . ."

ISSA KOBAYASHI (1763–1828). One of the three greatest traditional Japanese male haiku poets, along with Basho and Buson. As a Pure Land Buddhist, he espoused compassion for all living things, perhaps because he himself had a life of poverty and personal tragedy. See his autobiographical haibun collection, *Oraga Haru* (The Spring of My Life) from 1819.

this spring in my hut
there is nothing
there is everything

SODO YAMAGUCHI

I have always admired Mahatma Gandhi for living simply
with very few possessions: a loincloth, a comb, a watch, a
fountain pen, a notebook, and a copy of sacred Hindu
scriptures—that was about it. And Henry Thoreau, also
with only a few possessions, took up experimental living by
Walden Pond. But even they did not achieve ideal simplicity:
recent historical records show that Gandhi's simple lifestyle
was supported by other people's money and energy, and that
Thoreau went to Sunday dinners at his mother's house while
living at Walden. Yet both men knew the value of simplicity.
There is now a trend in postmodern cultures to reconsider
this value: to get away from rabid consumerism and get back

to simplicity. Most of us are weighed down by too much stuff, which is rooted in a consumer culture that emphasizes what we don't have rather than what we do have, which produces discontent. This is mental poverty; real poverty is a different story. This is not to romanticize real poverty at all, but an urging for all of us to live more simply and thus know more contentment. Whether or not the poet really did have "nothing," the haiku points the way to simplicity, feeling it is "everything" just to breathe in the spring air.

SODO YAMAGUCHI (1643–1716). Born in Kai and later moved to Edo (Tokyo), he became acquainted with Basho while studying with Kigin. He was respected by Basho, especially for his knowledge of Chinese classics.

13 · Interdependence

a heavy cart
rumbles by—
peonies tremble

BUSON YOSA

Peonies and humans are equals in the universe. Being part of the East Asian cultural tradition and a Buddhist priest when young, the poet understood this main tenet of interdependency: that the world of humanity and the nonhuman natural world are interwoven and not separate, that there are no separate selves, that humans are a part of Nature and not above it. This is deep ecological consciousness, that all are interconnected more than we realize; even modern physics now sees our planet and the universe as a web of dynamic interrelations. We can see it when we stop and notice even small things as the train rattles by, or the wind picks up, how the leaves on the trees are lifted, as well as the hairs on our head. We are touched and touch in return, every moment. This is the so-called "butterfly effect": that even the momentum caused by a butterfly moving its wings in the Amazon will be felt someday, somehow, somewhere—even in Paris or Cairo. It's hard to believe, but a truth we can all experiment with and observe every day. If we understand this, we cannot harm any living thing in the environment, for we are harming ourselves in the process, for there is no ultimate separation; we are all a part of this intimate cause and effect. This is the simple ecology of a peony trembling . . .

BUSON YOSA (1716–1784). One of the three greatest male haiku and renga poets (along with Basho and Issa), Buson was also a great painter of the literati art style and a master of vividly elegant images, which are evident in his haiku. He also illustrated Basho's haiku. Born in Osaka, he was at first a student of Kikaku, a close disciple of Basho. He later promoted the "back-to-Basho revival" that restored haiku to its former state. Some works include *Ake Garasu* (A Crow at Dawn) and *Shin Hanatsumi* (New Flower Picking).

the warbler poops
on the slender
plum branch

ONITSURA UEJIMA

Humor has always been a saving grace for the life dramas of
human beings and is supposedly one of our unique traits—
perhaps we have a humor gene in our DNA. It's been well
documented that laughing is not only good for the spirit but
good for bodily health: inner organs, cells, and especially the
heart. Humor cuts through our fixed thinking and brings a
fresh perspective so we can relax our mind and laugh. Not
cleverly joking at others, but genuinely sharing warmth.
Laughing from not taking ourselves so seriously for we know
that ultimately nothing is permanent or solid, including our
own thoughts and emotions. Actually seeing the illusory na-
ture of reality is cause for laughter, for we are relaxing with

the unknown and just seeing things in their naked state. My father expressed this another way, as something simple to follow. He would always tell me as a child, "Remember to laugh at yourself and cry for others," which is a good reminder to be open to others and not take ourselves so seriously. This haiku should change any preconception that haiku are only about "serious" things; haiku are always a witness to the surprising nature of things, however we find it, in the lightness of the moment: plum flowers, and oh! the droppings of a bird!

ONITSURA UEJIMA (1661–1738). His fame in Japan approached that of Basho. The son of a wealthy sake brewer, he began writing haiku as a child and studied with Kiin and Soin, both disciples of Shiko, who was a disciple of Basho. He uplifted haiku, using "sincerity" as the most important element, which was admired by Buson. His haiku is known for simplicity and earthiness, as expressed in his treatise on haikai, *Hitorigoto* (Talking to Myself), which was a best seller of 1718.

no flower can stay
yet humans grieve at dying—
the red peony

EDITH SHIFFERT

The truth of the way of Nature is not nice and cozy, but rather neutral and even tough. Anyone who has ever been stranded out in "wild Nature" quickly learns this fact; or anyone who has ever been in a natural disaster such as a flood or earthquake knows too well the unpredictable, unbiased nature of Nature. Another truth of Nature is that while it can be quite awesome, vulnerable, and beautiful, the beauty of a flower is not made for us: its fragrance, its color, its shape are the survival of its species. A prime example of this is the supposed "first flower" that was recently found in a rock fossil in southern China, the "arti fructus" from about 130 million years ago. The botanists said that the formation of the flower's beautiful petals and all were just the primordial expression of the flowering plant's better survival for the next passing generation. Above all, the truth of Nature is simply change and impermanence. We humans know that "no flower can stay," but we usually grieve about it—and yet, the poet who wrote this haiku in her eighties has accepted this impermanence, as perhaps a Taoist or Buddhist or as a flower—and there is nothing left to do but to be in and appreciate this way of Nature.

EDITH SHIFFERT (b. 1916). A foremost American haiku poet of her time, she is better known for her longer Imagist poetry. Kenneth Rexroth said, "her poetry possesses a reverence for life and gratitude for being, her being and all being." Born in Canada, she lived in Hawaii, Alaska, and, since 1963, in Kyoto, Japan, where she is known as a "cultural treasure." Her main works include *Kyoto Years, Clean Water Haiku* (with Minoru Sawano), *In the Ninth Decade,* and *Pathways.* Also, she was editor and co-translator, with Yuki Sawa, of *Haiku Master Buson* and the *Anthology of Modern Japanese Poetry.*

after the rain
bomb craters filled
with stars

JOHN BRANDI

There is a quote that has helped me for years, taken from the Buddhist text *The Sadhana of Mahamudra*: "good and bad, happy and sad, all thoughts vanish into emptiness like the imprint of a bird in the sky."[4] As much as we might dislike change when things are good and in our favor, we appreciate change when things are bad and not in our favor. How much more comforting it would be if we could, as in this quote, recognize that all things—whether good or bad, happy or sad—will ultimately fade, along with our thoughts and judgments of things, and that really on some level everything is coemergent. Usually this is not easy to see, but sometimes we can see this clearly when an incident occurs as in this poem: bombs creating craters where houses once stood and people once breathed and lived. Yet sometimes even within that destruction something else is occurring: rain and the stars' reflection within the destruction; the next morning the rain might be dried up by the sun and the stars' image gone too, like the fading "imprint of a bird in the sky" as it flies away into the distance. And we watch these things and our thoughts about these things arise and fade away...

JOHN BRANDI (b. 1943). At home in the New Mexican desert for years, from where he ran the Tooth of Times Press and sometimes ventured off to South America or Asia, Brandi enfolded his life encounters into thirty books. One of the leading American haiku poets as well as a travel writer (especially of haibun), he is also an editor, essayist, painter, and concerned activist. He received several awards, including a National Endowment for the Arts poetry grant. Among his works are *Weeding the Cosmos: Selected Haiku, In What Disappears,* and *Water Shining beyond the Fields.*

the shell i take
the shell it takes
ebb tide

VINCENT TRIPI

The brilliant natural magic of the world is here all the time. When everyday coincidences occur more and more as in this haiku, it is a sign that our mind is beginning to slow down, relax, and be in the present moment. When we are present our senses are more attuned to the environment and the environment to us. And we can let in and enjoy the subtle energy of the water taking the shell as we take it. Sakyong Mipham Rinpoche explains, "The world communicates to us because we're available, like a flower in spring. Conditions are ripe and the flower opens. Wisdom and compassion attune us to life, and the environment responds."[5] The environment is always presenting us with a new circumstance to learn from, be it a book, a shell, a lover, or a friend. The more we realize how everything is interrelated, and the more our minds are open, then the more auspicious our lives become. Not only to notice the ebb tide flowing around the shells, but to notice when all conditions are ripe in our lives: when it is time to act—to take a nature walk, to paint the house, or to have a child. Rinpoche sums it up: "Being present is where all power and magic lie." Whether in the city or at the seashore—there is magic to be found.

VINCENT TRIPI (b. 1941). One of the foremost American haiku poets, one living the "Way of Haiku" as a naturalist, as a Thoreau. He served as the head of the Haiku Poets of Northern California, but he now lives in the northwest woods of Massachusetts, where is he a part of a writing community whose members write from a spiritual perspective. He is also an editor and runs his own small press called tribe press. He is a prolific author of haiku books including *Haiku Pond: A Trace of the Trail and Thoreau, Tribe: Meditations of a Haiku Poet,* and *Snow Falling on Snow: A Collection of Poems about the Buddha,* and recently, *monk & i* and *paperweight for nothing.*

in the deep fires
I saw the way
a peony crumbles

SHUSON KATO

A peony crumbled, a skull cracked open, and the metal twisted in the fire's bloody explosion. It could be a suicide terrorist bomb attack; it could be a "shock and awe" air raid; it could be genocide in Darfur; it could be the Auschwitz death camp; it could be the Catholic Church's Inquisition, burning books and heretics; it could be the racist bombing of a Little Rock church; it could be the Ku Klux Klan burning crosses; it could be the bombing of Hiroshima; it could be any act of terrorism or violence throughout human history. Here the poet is depicting his experience of the air bombings of Tokyo in World War II, in which his house was burned down and he and his wife were separated from their children.

Whether it was a real peony or merely a metaphor, it is an unforgettable image of that incident, during which more civilians were killed than in the later atomic bombs. And so today we are left to ask ourselves, how can we face these terrible, fearful things? Perhaps by seeing the truth of the way it was and still is. Perhaps by knowing that fire does not quench fire. Perhaps by choosing not to be a part of—or sanction—this destructive cycle. Perhaps by standing up against violence in ourselves and others always, whether on a small scale or large. Perhaps by seeing the way a peony crumbles. Perhaps, someday, somehow.

SHUSON KATO (1905–1993). One of the great modern Japanese haiku poets, Kato was also a Basho scholar. In the 1930s he was associated with the Ashibi school of poetry and their magazine, founded by Shuoshi Mizuhara, which emphasized a humanist perspective. Later in the 1940s he founded the *Kanrai* (Thunder in Midwinter) journal, and a collection of his haiku uses the same title.

first light
everything in this room
was already here

CHRISTOPHER HEROLD

Nothing can hide from light—it touches everything equally, as does the sun and moon and stars beyond. Light is just there as the sky is there, as the earth and all the elements are there. This is sometimes referred to as "basic goodness" or "things just as they are," in their primordial natural state. Not good as opposed to bad, but "good" because it is unconditional, of the natural order. Sometimes we can see this and sometimes we can't; if we can, some sense of appreciation arises as in this poet's experience—in the light, finally seeing what was there all along—the absolute beauty of simplicity, of naked reality. It reminds me of an incident some years ago when my mother was released from the hospital after an operation and on the way home, though still weak, she looked out the car window and simply noted, "How pretty. Look at the sunlight against that brick wall." That was the same moment of appreciation. And perhaps that is also why we appreciate painters such as Vermeer, whose paintings of dark spaces are illuminated with a pure light; or Van Gogh's painting of the *Starry Night over the Rhone,* in which the energetic light from the brushed canvas pierces everything, including us. And we see again.

CHRISTOPHER HEROLD (b. 1948). A student of Shunryu Suzuki Roshi, he has been immersed in Zen practice and teaching for many years. One of the most prominent and active American haiku poets, his books of haiku include *Voices of Stone, In Other Words,* and *A Path in the Garden.* He is the editor of the international haiku journal *The Heron's Nest.*

picked
by an old woman's hand
herbs green and glowing

SOEN NAKAGAWA

This haiku poet, mostly known as a Zen master, said of his own haiku, "It represents a world where plus and minus are one . . . [a world] of absolute contradiction. To be dying is to be living, and to be living is to be dying. Death and life cannot be separated. They only have different names. . . . Here an old woman, a grandmother, is picking some herbs. As soon as she picks them, new shoots come up. I did not intend to create a haiku expressing the Zen viewpoint, but this is how things really are."[6] The same could be said of this world and the so-called spiritual world. It is all intertwined. Perhaps the most famous reference to this paradox is contained in the Prajnaparamita Hrdaya Sutra (Heart Sutra), where it is said:

"form is emptiness, emptiness itself is form."[7] It is not that the form is only material and the emptiness spiritual, but these two realms are *one,* and yet at the same time beyond one. And when we reflect upon it, something deep inside of us imperceptibly knows this truth but cannot speak it. So we are left with green herbs held in an old hand.

SOEN NAKAGAWA (1901–1984). One of the most famous and eccentric Zen masters of the twentieth century. He was the abbot of the historic Ryutaku monastery and a key figure in the transmission of Zen Buddhism from Japan to the Western world. Among his students were Eido Roshi (his dharma heir), as well as Robert Aitken and Philip Kapleau, who became two of the first Westerners to teach Zen in America. Nakagawa was also known for his dynamic calligraphy and haiku. See *Endless Vow: The Zen Path of Soen Nakagawa* by Kazuaki Tanahashi.

ah, in the corner
look again—
winter chrysanthemum, red

TEIJO NAKAMURA

The red of red. Chögyam Trungpa Rinpoche used to talk
about this in his Dharma Art and Poetics talks: the vivid-
ness of reality that is present each and every moment, if we
just stop and notice. To see what is here, without the need
to alter or gild our view of things. Every haiku is about this
"seeing," but this one in particular, written by a woman haiku
master whose haiku is known for its simple expression of the
everyday, reminds us "to simply see what is there"—a qual-
ity this poet told me was the key to haiku. The basic fabric
of reality is so brilliant that after a meditation retreat people
often comment that things look brighter, clearer, colors
more vivid; the color red has not changed, but our eyes have,

because our mind has dropped its preoccupation of thought and allowed a gap in which to see what is there. The "red wheelbarrow" of William Carlos Williams's famous poem, which further ignited the Imagist movement of the early twentieth century, epitomizes this. Noticing things, noticing colors as we are living and even dying; Rinpoche emphasized that sometimes even soldiers lying on a battlefield, wounded or dying, in those moments often tell of noticing, even appreciating, the color of the smoky red sky.

TEIJO NAKAMURA (1900–1988). One of the four *T*'s of the famous modern Japanese women haiku masters along with Takako Hashimoto, Tatsuko Hoshino, and Takajo Mitsuhashi. In the lineage of Shiki, she studied under Kyoshi who published her haiku in his *Hototogisu* (Cuckoo) magazine. She later had her own movement of women's haiku, as did Kyoshi's daughter, Tatsuko. Teijo's haiku group was Kazahana (Snow Flowers in Wind) and her books include *Teijo Haiku Collection* and *Red, White Plum*.

The taste
of rain
—Why kneel?

JACK KEROUAC

This "angel-headed hipster" wrote haiku and was passionately on a spiritual path, first as a Catholic boy and later as an explorer of Buddhism and Taoism. He was seeking what the ancients sought, what every human being seeks about her place in the universe. Although millions flock to churches, temples, and mosques, or embrace meditation practice or some ideology of science or religion, millions find or could find the sacred in the mystery of the everyday: in the rain, the call of a lark, the firefly in the night sky. In this seeming dark age we are more in need of a way, a simple practice connecting us to the "sacred," however we may find it, to bring us peace and aliveness. True to the Beat lineage of an "outrider," this haiku questions the traditional ritual of kneeling, for the poet finds enough prayer and sacredness in the "taste of rain." This is in tune with the popular Islamic saying, that "the whole world is a mosque,"[8] that one can pray and kneel anywhere. Yet the mystical Sufi tradition is closer to Kerouac, stating, "the world is but god veiled,"[9] so it doesn't matter if we are kneeling, standing, or dancing. The spiritual, the sacred, this very moment, being at one with the universe's energy, as in Kerouac's "golden eternity."

JACK KEROUAC (1922–1969). A Beat novelist and American cultural icon with a spontaneous prose style. In *On the Road* and other books he depicted the counterculture of the 1950s: sex, drugs, jazz, and Zen. He was also a lifelong experimenter of haiku (writing more than a thousand of them), after being introduced to it (as was Ginsberg) by Gary Snyder in 1955. He melded the Japanese tradition into "American haikus" and "pops"—the American free-syllabled haiku of three lines—recording these (1956–1966) in pocket notebooks, letters, and novels, of which five hundred are found in *Book of Haikus,* some in *Scattered Poems,* and as a recording of jazz and his haiku in, *Blues and Haikus.*

across a rose fence—
a cat lover
a cat hater

KAZUO SATO

This haiku reveals a poet who has a deep and wide perspective—one who can see far across the rose-hedge fence. Of all the haiku poets of modern Japan, Sato is the one who, in the last quarter of the twentieth century, contributed the most to the internationalization of haiku that Japan and other countries enjoy today. (I was fortunate to have him as my personal haiku mentor for ten years, which expanded my vision of haiku.) How important it is for all of us to be able to expand our vision beyond our own side of the fence, beyond our own personal likes and dislikes—feelings for and against, whether on an individual or national scale. For our overly protected boundaries are what lead to disharmony, disputes, and wars. The antidote is to be more like the rose hedge: neutral as nature, open to views from both sides of the fence and beyond. This microcosmic haiku exposes the truth of this sad absurdity of the world situation and yet it somehow nudges us to imagine, as in the classic John Lennon song, "Imagine" . . . and going beyond it.

KAZUO SATO (1927–2005). Modern Japanese haiku master and promoter of "world haiku." Early studies with the haiku translator R. H. Blyth sparked his interest. He was a professor, editor of "Haiku in English" for *Mainichi News,* a founder of Japan's Haiku International Association, and the head of the "International Section" of the Haiku Museum in Tokyo. His books include *Can Mustard Flower Be Transplanted?, Haiku Crosses the Sea,* and *From Haiku to Haiku,* as well as the haiku collection *And the Cat Too.* His awards include the Haiku Society of America's Lifetime Award and the Shiki International Haiku Prize.

saying nothing:
the guest, the host
the white chrysanthemum

RYOTA OSHIMA

High-tech cultures are moving at a speed unnatural to human beings, creating a wound of disconnection and discontentment deep within us. We are becoming creatures who can barely stand the sound of silence, of nothing happening. If we could but stop for a moment, if we could turn off the TV, computer, iPhone, or whatever gadget we are using, feel our breath moving through our lungs, smell the air, and see around us, we might be amazed by what we find. If we only do this five or ten minutes a day it could transform us. I remember, years ago in Korea in the Peace Corps, how I felt the first time I partook of the daily culture of "just sitting" together with friends in informal tearooms in Seoul, without saying a word; at first I felt quite nervous and bored, but when I was able to relax my mind and just be, it was a refreshing communion. This haiku depicts such a moment, yet a moment within the formal tea ceremony. Sen no Rikyu, the famed sixteenth-century Japanese tea master who was the founder of the art of tea and the ritualized tea ceremony of which silent communication is an essential part, coined the phrase, *ichi-go, ichi-e,* meaning "one time, one meeting." This became an integral part not only of the Zen arts but of everyday culture: since each moment's meeting of a person or even a flower is precious and fleeting, it is to be savored completely, perhaps best in silence.

RYOTA OSHIMA (1718–1787). A pupil of Ransetsu and one of the first of his generation to "rediscover" Basho. He was a prolific and influential haiku master of more than two hundred books and he had more than two thousand pupils, yet few of his poems remain. However, this one haiku is one of the best known out of all Japanese haiku. He recorded his ideas on haikai in *Basho Shichibu Sagashi* (Gleanings from the Seven Collections of Basho).

> stillness—
> piercing the rocks
> the sound of cicadas

BASHO MATSUO

Anyone who has heard the seventeen-year cycle when the cicadas return cannot help but hear their almost deafening sound. One hot summer, when visiting the northern mountainous region where Basho wrote this haiku—and where his haiku is chisled on a large rock, as is the Japanese custom—I could finally understand how the sound seemed to be literally piercing into the rocks. It's as if Nature is crying out for us to listen, like Georgia O'Keeffe's flowers, which she said she painted big and bright so we would really see them. Sometimes we need reminders to open our senses again, for the more we practice listening, the more we can hear. It was John Cage in 1952 who "shocked" people at the time by giving a now infamous music concert entitled "Four: 33." The audience heard no traditional concert music but rather the silence of the hall, which forced the audience into "listening" (for four minutes and thirty-three seconds) to the other "musical" sounds: someone coughing, a car driving by, the distant jet overhead, the sound of their own heartbeats. That was it, a lesson in listening to the music around us. We begin life listening to the sounds in the womb, and end our lives with hearing, the last faculty to shut down. And in between, there is so much to hear.

BASHO MATSUO (1644–1694). The greatest haiku poet in Japanese history. Coming from a low samurai class, he later became a renga master with many disciples, studied Zen, and traveled widely. He took haiku to a deeper level, espousing haikai no michi (the Way of Haiku) as a way of life and a return to Nature. See *Sarumino* (*Monkey's Raincoat,* a renga collection); and *Oku no Hosomichi* (*Narrow Road to the Interior,* a haibun collection). See also haiku translations in R. H. Blyth's *History of Haiku,* vol. 1 and Makoto Ueda's translation *Basho and His Interpreters*—just some among many translations.

Holding the water,
        held by it—
                the dark mud.

WILLIAM J. HIGGINSON

The word "Rashomonesque" has become a part of the English language and a part of our postmodern culture of Einsteinian relativism. In Akira Kurosawa's film *Rashomon*, taken from the haiku poet Akutagawa's original short story, we are shown a robbery in a forest through the flashbacks of four different persons' versions of the incident; and at the end of the film we are left wondering what is the real truth of what happened, which then provokes us to question our own sense of reality, and everyone else's, too. This well-known haiku addresses this dilemma—and yet leaves us with a feeling of embracing it all somehow: that we can hold and be held at the same time. It is leaping beyond dualistic thinking, and urging us to stretch our minds to see things from a wider view. It was the American expatriate and expert on Japanese culture Donald Richie, also an authority on Japanese film (especially Kurosawa), who said in an interview once that he didn't learn any "Zen enlightenment" from D. T. Suzuki (the promoter of Zen to the West), but he did learn "alternate ways of thinking,"[10] seeing things from multiple perspectives. And that would certainly suffice for most of us.

WILLIAM J. HIGGINSON (b. 1938). The leading American expert on haiku, a prominent haiku poet, a translator of Japanese haiku, and a liaison for international haiku. He was an editor of *Haiku Magazine* and the founder of From Here Press. He is also the author of major haiku texts and websites, including *The Haiku Handbook: How to Write, Share, and Teach Haiku* (coauthored with Penny Harter), *The Haiku Seasons: Poetry of the Natural World,* and *Haiku World: An International Poetry Almanac;* his own poetry collections include *Healing and Other Poems, Paterson Pieces, Death Is, Surfing on Magma,* and an e-book of translations of Japanese haiku called *Butterfly Dreams: The Seasons through Haiku and Photographs* with photographer Michael Lustbader.

pig and i spring rain

MARLENE MOUNTAIN

This is an American experimental haiku written in one line instead of three, yet it embodies the same elements by using only a few words. Most of all it embodies the quality of joy or delight in the coming of the awaited rainy season. Most haiku express a quiet appreciation for Nature, but this one expresses it with humorous exuberance. These days it seems it is hard for most of us to feel any kind of joy. Martin Buber, the Jewish theologian, insightfully said, "the beating heart of the universe is holy joy."[11] This would mean being able to find the divine in everything: the good and bad, just and unjust, beautiful and tawdry. A step further would be to find the divine in ourselves and others, in both our pain and joy.

I recall asking a Tibetan lama many years ago why I didn't feel any joy coming out of my meditation practice. He simply said that I had to think of others more by doing more *tonglen* practice (tonglen is a Tibetan meditation practice of imagining that one breathes in others' pain and breathes out well-being). It is a profound teaching and lifetime practice that I am grateful to have, and that could help all of us delight even in the rain with the pig.

MARLENE MOUNTAIN (b. 1939). A well-known American haiku poet hailing from Tennessee with her late haiku poet husband John Wills. She has devoted her life to haiku activities and other experimental, collaborative writing with other artists. She also practices nature photography and haiga-like ink sketches. Among her books are *Ada, OK: nature talks back* and *pissed off poems and cross words*.

farewell—
I pass as all things
the dew on grass

BANZAN

This simple haiku echoes the memorable Native American quote of the Lakota tribe, "Today is a good day to die, *hoka-hey* (all is completed)." It is indeed a courageous way to live and to die. It is quite a different approach than Welsh poet Dylan Thomas's equally memorable quote, "Do not go gentle into that good night / . . . Rage, rage against the dying of the light."[12] For most of us, one of these views or a melding of these two views are embraced at different times of our lives. Few of us can face old age, sickness, and death easily. However, a reflection to guide this process is to take a few minutes a day to think of each breath as if it were the last—each conversation, each taste of bread, as if it were the last one. And then see what arises, how we feel. Sometimes we might feel fear, sometimes sadness, or sometimes enjoyment or gratitude—or perhaps even a succession or mixing of these feelings. These moment to moment changes that once seemed unsettling, can become a way of seeing the fragility of it all, which just might then give rise to greater appreciation. For this exercise is not intended to be morbid, but a joyful one that invariably encourages us to live our lives more fully— to live a full life and a full death; to be able to say each and every day, "Today is a good day to die," for it just might be the last day. Hoka-hey!

BANZAN (1661–1730). A haiku poet of Basho's time. This haiku was written on the brink of his death, in the tradition of jisei, or "death haiku."

letting go
of a slanderous heart—
while shelling the beans

HOSAI OZAKI

Most haiku do not deal directly with emotions, since objectivity has been overly prized in haiku. Yet there are some haiku, like this unforgettable one, that cut to the bone of our emotional life. Dealing with our emotions is a hard practice: to honestly recognize that emotion we are feeling and then to let go of the emotion before it gets out of proportion, or to let go even if it is out of proportion already. However, this means neither suppressing nor acting out the emotion, but just acknowledging it for what it is. We need to remember that our so-called negative emotions are always workable. Just as each haiku gives us the birth and death of the moment, each moment gives us the birth and death of thoughts or emotions (which are said to be thoughts with energy attached to them), and we watch the "thoughts" rise, dwell and eventually fade away in a cycle again and again. Likewise, this haiku's everyday mini drama embodies the meditation practice of coming back to one's breath, no matter what thought or emotion happens to be raging inside of us. Just sitting at the kitchen table, mindfully coming back to the green beans: letting the shells slough off, letting our hardened shell of feelings slough off as well . . . bean by bean, breath by breath.

HOSAI OZAKI (1885–1926). A prominent modern Japanese haiku poet known for his "free verse" haiku. He studied with the haiku poet Seisensui Ogiwara when young. Later he studied law at Tokyo University and joined a company, but gave it up to become a beggar-monk living at temples in Kyoto. Before his only collection of haiku was published, he died of tuberculosis on an island alone in a humble hut. This is one of his most loved haiku in the *Oozora* (Big Sky) collection, written at Sumadera temple.

disgusting—
people arguing over
the price of orchids

SHIKI MASAOKA

Greed, once one of the seven deadly sins warned against in medieval Christian culture, has expanded through Western capitalism into the globalized culture of hyperconsumerism. Whether on an international or personal scale, it is difficult to switch our allegiance and notice the beauty of the pristine white orchids nodding in the hazy sunlight, and to realize the absurdity of wanting more and more. The poet here, even a hundred years ago in Japan, saw the same human axiom at work. Today this is a worldwide reality: when 1 or 2 percent of the world's people own most of the wealth and when the acquisition system of multinational corporations flowers on a world scale, the result is not just orchids that are at stake,

but the depletion of human and natural resources, result-
ing in plague, famine, war, and the ruin of the environment.
Only when human beings realize that everything on earth is
interdependent can we switch our thinking from competi-
tion to cooperation, from greed to compassion. Then we will
be able to just admire the orchids, perhaps together.

SHIKI MASAOKA (1867–1902). One of the four greats along with Basho,
Buson, and Issa, Shiki is considered the father of modern Japanese hai-
ku. He created "haiku" by totally cutting *hokku* (starting verse) from
the longer linked verse form of renga, and giving it a new name. He was
also a tanka poet and haiku theorist, espousing Buson over Basho and a
"sketch-from-life" style. He lived with tuberculosis and died young; his
haiku group's magazine was *Hototogisu* (Cuckoo). His works include
a diary titled *A Drop of Ink* and *Haiku Notebook of the Otter's Den;* his
disciples include the major poets Kyoshi and Hekigodo.

the homeless man
takes off his shoes before
his cardboard house

PENNY HARTER

The innate dignity of the human spirit, in spite of difficult circumstances: one only needs to recall Anne Frank's story of the Holocaust and how her personal diary written in a hideaway attic, not only uplifted her spirit but the spirits of millions who came after her. There is a word in Tibetan Buddhism, *lungta,* or *windhorse,* meaning "uplifted energy": something primordial within every living thing, which we can tap into anytime to refresh ourselves and uplift our spirits. It could be the simple act of lifting one's head even though depressed, opening a window to refresh the air, or taking off one's shoes to not dirty the floor. These small acts have more power and windhorse than we know; they can change our state of mind on the spot, and in accumulation become a whole way of life and thinking. At times we need to remind ourselves by consciously invoking this energy, anytime, anywhere: in the car, at work, or by our cardboard house. The Shambhala Buddhist teacher Cynthia Kneen clarifies: "Invoking windhorse is like raising a sail to catch and use the wind.... You can invoke it, tap it, tune into it, and ride it. Everyone without exception is born with personal dignity, power, and energy."[13] Likewise, this haiku is poignant because the "the homeless man" is viewed not as someone to ignore, revile, or to pity, but seen as just an ordinary human being who has lost something yet still maintains something deep within: that dignity which makes us truly human.

PENNY HARTER (b. 1940). Harter is one of the foremost American haiku poets, yet she writes mostly longer poetry. For years she has been a teacher and promoter of haiku in schools, and she is the coauthor (with William J. Higginson) of *The Haiku Handbook: How to Write, Share, and Teach Haiku.* She was also a former president of the Haiku Society of America. Her poetry books include *Turtle Blessing: Poems; Lizard Light: Poems from the Earth; Buried in the Sky;* and recently, *The Beastie Book,* a book for children; and a poetry collection *The Night Marsh.*

a petal falls

you

across the table

STEVE SANFIELD

In one of his talks, Chögyam Trungpa Rinpoche con-
founded the audience by calling relationships "the fast path."
Vajrayana Buddhism is known as the fast path: to get enlight-
enment in *one* lifetime. However, what most of us think of as
a spiritual path seems antithetical to our intimate relation-
ships, which often seem to be a distraction. Yet at the end of
the spiritual journey, as in the Zen oxherding paintings, the
herder has to return to the marketplace and be in the world,
in relation to others. Ultimately, of course, we are never out-
of-relationship, since we are interdependent, part of the
Hindu vision of the world and universe as "the net of Indra,"
in which each person is a jewel-point in each corner of the

net, reflecting all the other jewels. Knowing this, Rinpoche espoused a "fast approach" to this reality—that we see and work with our personal relationships as an opportunity for spiritual growth. This approach is "fast" because it is so intense, since we reflect each other and cannot hide who we really are when dealing with "the other" sitting across the table: the old raging father, the sad lover, or the whining child or cat. This very moment without escape: a petal falls, and there we are facing each other.

STEVE SANFIELD (b. 1940). A fine American haiku poet, at home in the foothills of the Sierra Nevada. Sanfield is a storyteller, folklorist, and editor of *Zero: A Journal of Contemporary Buddhist Life and Thought.* He was for years a student of the late Zen master Joshu Sasaki Roshi. His collections of poetry include *A New Way, Only the Ashes,* and *Crocuses in the Snow.* He calls these poems "hoops" rather than "haiku" because they include the "season of the heart," as in the Native American's sacred hoop or circle.

on the patio
the afternoon drifts along
with the butterfly

PATRICIA J. MACHMILLER

This haiku perfectly reflects a lazy summer afternoon. But this is really *not* lazy; to take time out is healing and necessary, especially in our postmodern world of speed. As I take out the garbage, I am grateful to the butterfly—rare these days with increasing endangered species, to even see a white butterfly—and I am grateful to the butterfly, to pause and watch it dart freely and relaxed in the humid air, for it is a reminder for me to rest as well, to refresh myself; my spirit needs a Sabbath. To have a moment of not looking at the clock, to drop our problems and busy agendas and to reconnect to the eternal time and space that is ever present. We need more leisure time of doing absolutely nothing—not vacation time, but just napping in a hammock, staring at the tiger lilies, or breathing with a butterfly. For in the speed of modern culture, instead of using saved time to be quiet, to sit still and just be, we instead do another thing—go to another appointment, travel a farther distance, and wonder why we have less time. Our modern litany is, "I don't have enough time." Speed accelerates, draws us into the vortex, so instead of doing less we are doing more. This has a dehumanizing effect and defeats our original purpose, which is to have more time to relax and enjoy doing nothing, drifting with the butterfly . . .

PATRICIA J. MACHMILLER (b. 1941). A prominent American haiku poet and member of the Yuki Teikei Haiku Society (based in California), which adheres to the traditional 5-7-5 syllable count in English. She served as the society's president for some years. She is a disciple of the late Kiyoko Tokutomi and her husband, Kiyoshi Tokutomi. Machmiller is a coeditor, along with June Hopper Hymas, of *Young Leaves: 25th Anniversary Issue of* Haiku Journal. She also writes a haiku column for the journal *Geppo* with Jerry Ball. Her main haiku collection is *Blush of Winter Moon.*

after the riot—
such a perfect
moonlit night

HEKIGODO KAWAHIGASHI

To see things with a vast view: to see that everything in the universe is in flux, in process of changing. To quote Thich Nhat Hanh, the Vietnamese meditation master, "Everything is in transformation. The rose that wilts after six days will become a part of the garbage. After six months the garbage is transformed into a rose. When we speak of impermanence, we understand that everything is in transformation."[14] This haiku reflects this universal change.

The moon in East Asia is a symbol for enlightenment, for vast vision, as it pervades the night sky shining equally upon all things: riot or no riot. We need to keep our perceptions open; if we can transform our perceptions, then all transforming things become vivid in our eyes. Saint Exupery's *Little Prince* points the way, "it is only with the heart that one can see rightly; what is essential is invisible to the eye."[15] If seen in this vast light, nothing needs to be rejected—the riot or the moon—for it is all a part of the transformation process. This haiku is a luminous distillation of our human life, seen deeply with the eyes of the heart.

HEKIGODO KAWAHIGASHI (1873–1937). A famous Japanese modernist poet and one of the two main disciples (along with Kyoshi) of Shiki, the father of modern haiku. Kawahigashi was an experimenter, advocating "free verse" haiku without a 5-7-5 syllable count. He was also editor of *Nippon Haiku* magazine. His main haiku collection is *Shinkeiko Kushu,* and his disciples included Seisensui and Ippekiro. In addition to writing haiku, he was a newspaper reporter, Noh dancer, calligrapher, mountain climber, and haiku critic.

migrating birds—
fields of pampas grass
show the way

KRISTEN DEMING

We humans think our way of communicating is unique, but the more we study other species, we realize they are communicating on a deeper level than we know, as mirrored in this haiku. There is a theory about this called "Hundredth Monkey Effect," based on studies of monkeys conducted in the nineteen fifties by Japanese scientists on Koshima Island. The monkeys were observed eating sweet potatoes dug from the ground, with dirt still clinging to them, until one day one monkey washed his potato in the ocean; other monkeys saw and followed suit until about a hundred monkeys were doing it. At that point, spontaneously, to everyone's surprise, the scientists found that colonies of monkeys on other islands farther away began washing their potatoes, too. This provoked the idea of there being a powerful level of awareness that could be tapped into to change ways of thinking. It is not prayer particularly, but rather a vast field of consciousness. Some visionaries such as Ken Keyes have used this monkey study to show the powerful possibility to change the world's focus from war to peace and, most of all, from a nuclear to a nonnuclear world. The hope is, if more people think about peace, then the "thought energy" of shared awareness could pervade the world, like the hundredth monkey's realization, and someday become a reality. As embodied in this haiku's image, if the tall silver pampas grass bending in sunlight could show the way without saying a word, couldn't humans as well show the way?

KRISTEN DEMING (b. 1939). One of the foremost American haiku poets as well as a renku (group linked verse) poet. Deming served as president of the Haiku Society of America and lived in Japan for some years with her husband, who was the DCM and acting American ambassador. While in Japan she was the English consultant for *Tomoshibi* (Light), the collected tanka of the emperor and empress of Japan; she was also a guest at the New Year's Poetry Party at the Imperial Court. As a promoter of haiku and renku, she is like an ambassador of haiku worldwide. A collection of her haiku is *Eyes of the Blossoms*.

The gull
giving loneliness
sound.

ALEXIS ROTELLA

Loneliness is the emotion most often expressed in haiku, if any. Perhaps it is because aloneness is our primordial state in birth and death and much of the time in between. This haiku's sparseness expresses "loneliness" through space: the vast beach and vaster sky—and then the piercing cry of the gull. Sometimes being alone can be a time to refresh ourselves in the positive sense of aloneness, in which we can relax, feel our innate connection to Nature, part of vast, breathing Gaia. However, Mother Teresa, the renowned Christian nun working for the poor in India, noted after visiting America that the greatest illness in the West was *loneliness,* accompanied by a spiritual vacuum. Perhaps she was referring to a loneliness coming from alienation, not realizing that we are interdependent with everything, and ultimately not separate. Perhaps she was referring to a loneliness coming from individualistic gratification, and forgetting about others. Perhaps she was referring to a loneliness coming from a loss of community and thus a disconnection from others. In this regard, what impressed me about India when I visited was how people were ususally sitting together engaging with each other, whether indoors or outdoors, in the city or countryside; there was a deep sense of the communal, almost a communion feeling. Perhaps it's something we've lost, and loneliness is the result; it's something to be aware of, something to think about, the next time we feel lonely on an empty beach.

ALEXIS ROTELLA (b. 1947). A prominent American haiku poet who writes *senyru* as well, giving "revelations of emotional relationships" with herself and the world. She also served as president of the Haiku Society of America and is widely published in prominent haiku journals. A recent haiku collection of hers is *Sassy.*

Ever lingering
in the taste of the walnut:
deep autumn.

JAMES W. HACKETT

Eating food is ordinary, yet it is our most important primor-
dial, almost sensual activity. Of the five senses, in haiku taste
is not often or easily captured, but it is here with Nature's en-
tire autumn season found in the nutshell of a walnut's taste.
Every day when we taste and eat food, whatever our choices,
we could acknowledge it with a prayer, bow, or silent thanks,
that this is a sacred act by a sacred person of a sacred plant
or sacred animal in the web of life; and above all, remember
that we, too, are a part of the food chain, and will be Nature's
meal someday. A Vietnamese saying reminds us further that
when eating fruit, think of the person who planted the tree.
We could also reflect upon the food chain and elements that

73

came together to deliver this walnut: the sun and water for the soil and tree growth; the wind, insects, and birds to carry the seeds; the gardener to tend to the tree; the picker of the nuts—and if we're a consumer rather than a farmer, we remember the driver of the truck to the marketplace or factory where it is packaged by many hands and sent to the store: the endless chain to place the walnut in our palm and mouth so we can taste and remember this sacred act.

JAMES W. HACKETT (b. 1929). A pioneering and prominent American haiku poet. His haiku first appeared in the 1960s in the appendix to R. H. Blyth's *History of Haiku,* as examples of haiku written in English. A lecturer on haiku and judge of haiku, his main works include *The Zen Haiku and Other Zen Poems of J. W. Hackett* and, recently, *That Art Thou: My Way of Haiku.*

a sparrows' nest
perhaps
inside the A-bomb dome

KINICHI SAWAKI

Hiroshima: the power of that one word. Remembering Hiroshima on August 6, over sixty years later, I am alarmed that there is no news of it today in the U.S. media, a day that should be "world peace day," with humanity's vow not to repeat this devastation. I only hope future readers live in a nonnuclear world. I remember my first pilgrimage to Hiroshima years ago, crying and thinking that every world leader must visit this sacred place—that their experience would be profound and they would call for a nuclear-free world. Is this an illusion, or is it an illusion to need deterrent weapons, for someday one of the thousands of nuclear bombs (each a thousand times the power of the first A-bomb) might be unleashed. The image I remember in Hiroshima that personalized this for me was the burned, outlined shadow of an unknown man heat-imprinted on stone steps, which were once part of a bank building he was about to enter when the light of the bomb flashed that morning at 8:15 A.M. and he disappeared. The other equally haunting image is the one expressed in this haiku: the black dome shell of a building, the only one left standing after the A-bomb exploded above it; it is now preserved by UNESCO as a symbol of peace to remember Hiroshima. Here, the haiku image of the A-bomb dome becomes poignant with the simple image of the new life emerging from within the dome, from within the nest of Nature's small sparrows . . . perhaps such a vision is possible, perhaps.

KINICHI SAWAKI (1919–2001). A prominent modern haiku poet. His wife Ayako Hosomi was also a well-known poet. Sawaki was the leader of the Kaze (Wind) group for years. He also served as president of the Association of Haiku Poets in Japan. Among his works is a treatise on Basho titled *Oku no Hosomichi Wo Aruku* (Walking the Narrow Road to the Deep North). Two of his haiku collections are *Yukishiro* (White Snow) and *Enden* (Salt Farm).

drawing light
from another world—
the Milky Way

YATSUKA ISHIHARA

A meteor shower tonight over Chicago—the sky too bright with city lights and white clouds, but then I detect a few pale streaks across the night sky and my heart quickens. The heavens, the eternal mystery since humankind emerged on this planet, as we float through the galaxies and possible multiverses, riding on the arm of our spiraling Milky Way galaxy. As quoted in verse one of the Chinese classic the *Tao Te Ching*, "the Tao that can be spoken is not the true Tao." We are left wondering the eternal question of life's origin and purpose: did meteor showers and comets of ice bring water and life forms to planet Earth millions of years ago? Was there an intervention by "gods," intelligent extraterrestrials

77

from another world, visiting this planet aeons ago? Is there a transcendent higher power or creative force, called by different names: God, Allah, the Great Spirit, Atman, God Within, Buddha Nature, the Tao, Divine Love, Cosmic Energy, the Mystery? Something within human beings feels fearfully in awe of this mystery, yet yearns for it. Seeing the Milky Way is a rare chance to experience this, yet not many people, especially in cities, do anymore. Perhaps there should be sacred pilgrimages to planetary spots like "Milky Way Center Retreats" where we could see the Milky Way in its entire vividness, from some island or mountaintop where the lights of civilization cannot reach. Then like the poet of this haiku we could gaze up at the luminosity, knowing ours is but one of billions of stars in billions of galaxies, among billions of beings . . . and we could breathe in the starlight, knowing that "the stars are in our bones."

YATSUKA ISHIHARA (1919–1998). A revered contemporary Japanese haiku master whose group's name is Aki (Autumn). His teachers were Dakotsu Iida and Tatsuji Miyoshi. The author of over forty books of haiku, literary criticism, and essays, Ishihara was a haiku lecturer, contest judge, and advisor. His haiku theory was "introspective shaping," looking inward as well as outward. Translations of his haiku appear in *Red Fuji*, translated by Tadashi Kondo and William J. Higginson with an introduction by Kristen Deming. His famous "Milky Way haiku" was carved into a "poem stone" (*kuhi*) in 1995.

> splitting
> the stone of a white peach
> with the edge of the knife

TAKAKO HASHIMOTO

The well-trained samurai approach—to cut swiftly and cleanly without hesitation. Basho advocated this approach to haiku: to go beyond hesitation, "like biting a pear or cutting into a watermelon, that there should be no time between the inception of the haiku moment and the expression of it."[16] This haiku was written by a woman who dared many things in her daily life and brought that quality to her haiku. Perhaps we, too, in our life could more often take a leap, to move beyond postmodern ambivalence, to take a stand and act: whether it be regarding close family and friends or for the social and political causes we believe in. To be a Joan of Arc, unafraid to cut though something when needed and to hone the skillful means necessary to do it. Trungpa Rinpoche advised how to work with this in our own meditation practice, a practice that involves cutting any subtle ego attachment: to cut thoughts, however gently, and discipline oneself not to indulge the mind and follow every meandering thought, but rather return to the clean and open breath, like the sky, like the clean stone of the peach.

TAKAKO HASHIMOTO (1899–1963). One of the great modern woman haiku masters, one of the four *T*'s of Japanese haiku. She first studied with Hisajo Sugita, the infamous woman haiku master. Later she studied with Kyoshi and Seishi Yamaguchi. Hashimoto was associated with the Hototogisu and Ashibi haiku schools, but later with Seishi formed the *Tenro* (Heaven) school and magazine, which still exists today. Her main works include *Umi Tsubame* (Sea Swallows), *Beniito* (Red Thread), and *Myoju* (The End of Life). She received the Nara Cultural Prize in 1959.

moonlight—
through thin clothes
to naked skin

HISAJO SUGITA

To be vulnerable, to let the world touch us—be it a person or
moonlight. To let it touch us deeply is almost sensual, almost
as if becoming *one* with the Mystery with our whole body
and spirit. Actually this haiku has a mythological reference,
taken from the ancient Japanese text of the *Nihonshoki*, of
the Soto Ori Hime Princess who was known for her beauti-
ful skin which was said to shine through her clothes. Here
the moonlight, too, makes the poet's skin perhaps luminous
as well. Unlike any other haiku about the moon, this haiku,
written by a so-called "eccentric" woman poet, expresses
not an ordinary viewing of the moon and feeling it in her
heart, but as if tactilely feeling it on her whole body, under

her clothes down to her naked skin. People talk about bathing in sunlight but rarely in moonlight, and never moonlight through clothes. In modern Japan, there is a Japanese-English term called "skin-ship" between people who are close, be it family, friends, or lovers—those that you have taken a bath with, like at the public bath or hot springs, immersed in hot water, naked together in silence or soft talking, communing with the elements, back to a primordial state. It is a feeling of being at home, without shame or censure, relaxed in our vulnerability down to our naked skin.

HISAJO SUGITA (1890–1946). A prominent modern Japanese woman haiku master. Sugita was a passionate woman who became a teacher among women haiku poets of the Hototogisu (Cuckoo) school under Kyoshi. She went on to found her own magazine, *Hanagoromo* (Flowered Kimono). She was later dismissed from her school for her eccentricity; she supposedly became insane and died thereafter. After her death, her power as a poet became more recognized.

shown a flower
the small baby
opens its mouth

SEIFU-NI

The fragile and delightful breath of new life, captured in baby portraits worldwide, as in this intimate haiku. No matter their background—their country, city, village, or whether rich or poor—all babies hold the same fragility and innocence. But it's an innocence that needs protection, and not just the protection of the mother and family, but the world family at large. For it is the children who suffer the most in wars, genocide, famine, and epidemics. Calling for our attention are the innocent eyes of child refugees or just a baby's tiny mouth yearning for sustenance, even if from a flower, as in this haiku.

There is a Zen story of Buddha's "flower sermon,"[17] given

to all of his disciples, in which he just held up a single flower without saying a word—supposedly only one disciple, Mahakashyapa, smiled and understood. Perhaps this baby is one who also understood when it opened its mouth just so. To understand and be open to life and delight in it, we need the innocence of a child, as Jesus says in the Christian Bible, "Unless you become like a child, you cannot enter the kingdom of heaven."[18] And so says Basho, the most famous haiku poet, that we must have the eyes and heart of a child to really see the world. We need to protect this innocence of children and also that child within ourselves.

SEIFU-NI (1731–1814); her family name was Enomoto. One of the greatest traditional Japanese woman haiku poets. She belonged to the Basho-revival school and was the main female disciple of Shirao Kaya, yet studied first with Chosui. Born into a samurai family; learned haiku from her stepmother. After the death of her husband and later her teacher, Shirao, she became a Buddhist nun at the age of sixty and practiced Zen meditation at a temple in Kamakura. Her son published a poetry collection of her five hundred haiku, *Seifu-ni Kushu*.

in dreams
and in awakening—
the color of the iris

SHUSHIKI

The dreamlike quality of life. The blue iris glinting in the sun in my grandmother's garden when I was eight; me in the photograph pointing to the flower as if yesterday—a moment beyond time and space, like a dream. As we get older the past and present seem more intertwined and dreamlike. Some cultures, as in traditional Japan, believed one could meet a lover in a dream; in traditional Balinese culture night dreams were another plane of reality shared with the family in the morning; in aborigine Australian culture "dreamtime" exists alongside everyday reality. Most cultures hold dreams as something mysterious: a portent of things to come, an interpretation of things past. Throughout history, dreams remain an enigma, though we have the psychology of Jungian archetypes and Freudian innuendos of modern culture; and though modern science finds a physical and emotional necessity for dreams, it doesn't fully understand them. Buddhism suggests that "life be regarded as a dream"—that this state of so-called "awake reality" is no different from the "dream reality." To this point, Chuang Tzu, the ancient Chinese Taoist philosopher, questioned whether he was a man dreaming he was a butterfly or a butterfly dreaming he was a man. This is not to deny our awake state, but to see the fleeting, ephemeral quality of it and thus be less attached to our personal desires and more open and appreciative of our life. This *jisei* (death haiku), written right before she died, reflects an enlightened view: that the vividness of the iris's blueness remains, just as it is, beyond awake, beyond dreaming, beyond our understanding, that there is but one color, one reality.

SHUSHIKI (1668–1725); her family name was Ome. One of the foremost Japanese women haiku poets of her time. From an early age the student of Kikaku Takarai, Basho's favorite disciple; her husband, Kangyoku, was also a teacher of haiku. Shushiki was best known for this haiku at the age of thirteen: "watch out / drunk with sake— / that cherry tree by the well."

Full winter moon:
the icicle
the icicle's shadow

GERALDINE CLINTON LITTLE

The sun and moon; light and dark; order and chaos; male
and female; the Madonna and the whore; good and evil; life
and death: a set of primordial opposites existing within ev-
erything in the yin-and-yang balance of the universe. Yet as a
reminder that part of each exists within the other, the dot of
the opposite color is in the center of the black and white yin-
and-yang symbols. Sometimes it's more difficult to see the
shadow side than the light, because it's something we don't
want to acknowledge or see. Yet how liberating to finally see
it: "For now we see through a glass darkly; but then face to
face"[19] as in the Biblical quote. The irony in this haiku is that
everything is clear in the light of the full moon, and crystal

clear in the winter, yet the light of the moon is coming from the reflected light of the sun, its opposite, its shadow so to speak—and *that* is the light creating the shadow, its opposite: an encapsulation of opposites through this one image. If we look deeply, we can see this dynamic at work in everything around us and in ourselves. This personal shadow, however, is the most difficult to embrace. All the wise ones such as Saint Francis of Assisi suggest that we "love the leper inside."[20] To be able to face and name our shadow demons and learn from our imperfections, whether hatred, selfishness, or insecurity—to accept these is actually a challenging spiritual practice. It is usually easier for us, whether individuals or nations, to demonize so-called "enemies" and blame things on others, instead of looking deep within to our icicle's shadow.

GERALDINE CLINTON LITTLE (1924–1997). Originally from Ireland, Little was one of the best known and active American haiku poets of her generation, even though she didn't start writing until her mid-forties. She served as president of the Haiku Society of America. Among her works, which include free verse and sonnets as well as haiku, are *Star-Mapped* and *Woman in a Special House*.

bright sun
the sheen of tall grass
when it bends

JIM KACIAN

Within the Japanese Shinto tradition, all of nature is sacred and imbued with a spirit called a *kami*. Every rock, tree, and blade of grass has a spirit. This exists in most so-called ancient, indigenous, spiritual traditions worldwide. However, this tradition goes even further, that this spirit is inherent not just in animate things, but also in inanimate things. This was revealed to me while residing in Japan and opening up a newspaper one morning to see a photo of office workers in a Tokyo firm, standing lined up, dignified and bowing: bowing to the old machines that were being taken out and being replaced by new ones—thanking them for their good service. That is a "sacred outlook": to be able to see the sacredness or spirit within everything in our world without discrimination. Yet if we think carefully about the components of a machine, it is made of things originally of the natural world: the metals and crystals, the electric current, the plastics, the cardboard and all the invisible electrons in motion. The "sheen of tall grass" in this haiku embodies the same sacred outlook that was memorably recorded in Walt Whitman's revered *Leaves of Grass*. And like the view of the machine, this outlook could be extended to the sheen of a glass window or the sheen on our spoon at breakfast. This view of the world is lacking in our high-speed culture where sacred outlook is often forgotten. The trend of crass consumerism and hyped pop culture ignores the "sheen of tall summer grass." And if we forget this, we also forget the sacredness within ourselves.

JIM KACIAN (b. 1953). A prominent and active American haiku poet. For years he has been the editor and poetry publisher of Red Moon Press. A recent poetry collection of his is *Six Directions: Haiku and Field Notes.*

not seeing
the room is white
until that red apple

ANITA VIRGIL

The apple in this haiku is not Eve's apple of "knowledge," but just an ordinary apple whose red color becomes a catalyst of change to see more expansively: the white room. Contrast is another means to awaken us out of habitual ways of looking at the world. Most haiku are based on this principle, as is this haiku, of seeing the small against the large or one thing against another, as in these famous examples: the Milky Way seen through the tiny paper hole of a window; a tiny butterfly asleep on a huge temple bell. Even major historical events are often seen in a vaster light when a catalyst emerges—what comes most to mind is an image from 1963 that is burned into the collective conscience of everyone who saw it in the newspaper, magazine, or on television: that image of Thich Quang Duc, the Vietnamese monk who in protest against the Vietnam War immolated himself in a Saigon square by pouring gasoline on himself and lighting a match, as he sat still in a meditation position till he was black ash. That moment was a turning point: people could not help but awaken more deeply to what was happening in Vietnam and what the world was or was not doing about it. The red apple was on fire—and that is something impossible to ignore.

ANITA VIRGIL (b. 1931). One of the earliest, most prominent, and most active American haiku poets. Virgil was president of the Haiku Society of America in 1973. She is also an artist who gives art exhibitions of her sparse haiku-like drawings. Her poems, reviews, and essays appear in haiku magazines in the U.S. and overseas. Some of her collections are *One Potato Two Potato Etc., A 2nd Flake,* and *Pilot.*

for Allen Ginsberg

MAROON
suitcase
by
a
garbage can.
My
white
breath
in
air

MICHAEL MCCLURE

This haiku is dedicated to his close Beat poet friend, Allen Ginsberg, who was in the tradition of the Imagists—and especially of William Carlos Williams who was the spokesperson who led the way, along with haiku translations in the early twentieth century—to embrace the *image* as the whole poem as in the well-known edict: "no ideas but in things" à la the "maroon" wheelbarrow. However, McClure, always pushing the limits of literary possibilities as in this concrete haiku, has created another layer by including how the placement of the black-inked words look on the space of white paper, just as the Zen masters do with their splash of black-inked calligraphy. This haiku expresses "the ordinary" as all haiku try to do, but encapsulates it in a cloud of breath, giving it life, so we see what has been there/*here* all along. Everything is stripped down to its naked state without adornment to, as he says, its "energy constructs." Just us human beings breathing by an abandoned suitcase by a garbage can, on the "haiku edge" of perception.

MICHAEL MCCLURE (b. 1932). A prominent American poet who also experiments with haiku. McClure was a key figure in the San Francisco Renaissance of the 1950s, which was associated with the Beats. McClure is an experimenter of words and a collaborative performer with musicians such as Ray Manzarek. He is the author of over thirty books, some recent ones being *Rain Mirror* and *Plum Stones.*

lily:

out of the water . . .

out of itself

NICHOLAS VIRGILIO

This haiku is a favorite to many, perhaps because it is mercurial. Yet it points to the inner nature of every living thing: our roots. Unlike our ancestors, in this speedy mobile world, we do not stay long enough in one place to make roots—much less to make a garden or even to remember where we came from. The Native American Luther Standing Bear's astute observation of Americans over a hundred years ago could apply today: "The roots of the tree of life haven't grasped the rock and the soil. . . . man must be born and re-born to belong. Their bodies must be formed of the dust of their ancestors' bones."[21] Likewise, on a greater scale, we are just beginning to realize the uprooting power of globalization, especially to human beings' culture, communities, and the land. Rumi, the thirteenth-century Islamic Persian poet, lamented this loss in his *Song of the Reed Flute:* "Listen to the reed . . . how it sings of separation: / Ever since they cut me from the reed bed my cry has caused weeping . . . / Whoever has been parted from his source longs to return to the state of union."[22] He was speaking of a mystical union with the Divine, but it could be a union with the roots within ourselves, with our culture and community, with our ancestors, or with Nature. The alienation of modern peoples worldwide, whether refugee victims of war and famine, or developing countries' victims of slick globalization or consumer victims of hyperliving, is all rooted more than we realize, in this rootlessness. We need to remember and get back to roots, if only in small ways, to somehow keep that tenuous thread, of the root of the lily.

NICHOLAS VIRGILIO (1928–1989). One of the foremost pioneering American haiku poets. A lecturer and promoter of haiku in universities, radio and television programs, and haiku festivals. Ironically, he died of a heart attack while taping an interview on haiku for *The Charlie Rose Show* for PBS in 1989. His haiku is in Harold Henderson's classic, *Haiku in English;* his last collection of haiku was *Selected Haiku.*

morning glories—
the well-bucket entangled
I ask for water

CHIYO-NI

The great heart of compassion: to ask for water at her neighbor's house rather than disturb the flower. To not have strict boundaries of *self* and *other*—to be able to see from the eyes of a flower. However, kindness has two faces: remembering kindness to others and remembering others' kindness to us; ultimately they are one and the same, as we are interdependent. The Buddhist teaching on this feels overwhelming at first: "all human beings have been our *mother* before (in other lifetimes)." This could be extended to include *all* sentient beings such as the morning glory, but just thinking of other humans is a challenging first step: to respond with kindness to all our "mother beings" by remembering we are that closely connected and not separate. The Zen scholar D. T. Suzuki sees this signature haiku of Chiyo-ni's as an expression of this enlightened view and compares it to Basho's famous frog haiku: "Basho's frog produced a sound jumping into the old pond, and this gave him a chance to commune with the spirit of . . . Eternity itself. In Chiyo-ni's case it was the morning glory . . . the perfect identification between subject and object, seer and seen . . . she was not conscious of herself. . . . Her mind was filled with the flower, the whole world turned into the flower, she was the flower itself."[23] Since Chiyo-ni was a Jodo-Shinshu nun, her vow was not to harm anything, even the tiniest part of Nature. This remembering to be kind, even to the flower, is the refrain of the fourteenth Dalai Lama's religion, which he says anyone can simply practice on the spot, remembering "flower mind."

CHIYO-NI (1703–1775), or Kaga no Chiyo; her family name was Fukumasuya. One of the greatest traditional Japanese women haiku poets. Born into a scroll maker's family, she studied with two of Basho's disciples, was a renowned renga master, painter, and Buddhist nun. She published two poetry books: *Chiyo-ni Kushu* (Chiyo-ni's Haiku Collection) and *Matsu no Koe* (Voice of the Pine). Known for living Basho's "Way of Haiku." See *Chiyo-ni: Woman Haiku Master* by Patricia Donegan and Yoshie Ishibashi.

he says a word
I say a word:
autumn deepens

KYOSHI TAKAHAMA

This haiku has a mysterious quality. Out of the silence of the Void came life, consciousness, sound, and the naming of the ten thousand things: in words. The first oral storytellers of every ancient culture were thought to be shamans who carried the sacred mission of touching the Mystery: the sacred words, of more than so-called myths, were told around the fires of caves, and later the *Rig Veda,* the *Epic of Gilgamesh,* the *Odyssey, Popul Vuh,* and the *Kojiki,* to name a few—were all magical words before they were written down. This haiku epitomizes this ordinary, extraordinary happening: the temporal and the eternal coming together as one, in the moment of speaking a word . . . Supposedly a baby's first cry is the sound of *ah*, the beginning of the primordial sound: the seed syllable *om* in Sanskrit. It is said to embody the energy of the whole universe, of which everything is a manifestation. If we break down the syllable *om* into its component sounds, *ah-o-m* and *om* are equivalent: the *ah* (from back of the mouth) is the birth; the *o* (in the middle of the mouth) is the coming into being; and the *m* (in the front of the mouth) is the completion. And at the end of the *om*, there is only silence which it came out of and goes back into: here the atmosphere of an autumn day deepening. The sound of *om* puts us in touch with the universe, found in religious songs and chants, but also found in every sound, in almost every word that we speak, if we are aware and in dialogue with words, with the other; if we can feel each word and the space around each word—and then each brush of cool wind, each leaf dropping, as autumn dusk descends.

KYOSHI TAKAHAMA (1874–1959). The most influential Japanese haiku poet and critic of his time. Forgoing higher education, he set up a firm to publish haiku books. He was a prolific writer of haiku (tens of thousands), many of which appear in *Kyoshi Kushu* (Collected Works of Kyoshi), and also of novels, short stories, and essays. After his teacher Shiki's death, as a main disciple Kyoshi took over *Hototogisu* (Cuckoo), which is still carried on by his granddaughter, Teiko Inahata (b. 1931). He also influenced many well-known haiku poets of following generations.

summer grasses—
the wheels of a locomotive
come up to a stop

SEISHI YAMAGUCHI

This haiku was written by one of the first modernists to use contemporary imagery in Japanese haiku; yet he was still insistent upon using a kigo, or Nature reference, in all haiku. I was fortunate to study with him when he was in his late eighties—and I learned this lesson well, for he would not look at my haiku if they lacked a reference to Nature. This haiku is a distillation of this view, for the iron locomotive is almost bowed in front of Nature's "summer grasses"—Nature being the umbrella for all human life and every living thing. We've all had the experience of walking down the street and noticing the cracks in the sidewalk, from which green grass is sprouting—Nature being the primary "civilization" beyond the human realm. Just thinking of the Seven Wonders of the World—all that is left is one remnant: the oldest and largest, the pyramids that are still in the process of returning to dust as well. And even the one human-made structure visible from space, the Great Wall of China, is also crumbling. It is easy to forget in our postmodern "civilization" that these monuments of human beings—skyscrapers, cathedrals, and mosques; highways and bridges; and high-tech implements of both war and peace—are ultimately made up of Nature's elements of metal, glass, stone, wood, and fibers, which will eventually return to Nature. Perhaps the so-called "uncivilized" natural or indigenous peoples, who leave fewer traces, and no carbon footprints, may be in the end the wisest and most civilized.

SEISHI YAMAGUCHI (1901–1994). One of the four S's (along with Shuoshi, Seiho, and Suji), who were the Japanese haiku giants of the twentieth century. Yamaguchi was a main disciple of Kyoshi. He advocated a modern approach to haiku themes and "an imagination jump," but adhered to the 5-7-5 form and kigo (season word). His group and magazine *Tenro* (Heaven) flourishes today. He wrote haiku essays, taught haiku widely, and edited haiku for newspapers. See *The Essence of Modern Haiku: 300 Poems by Seishi,* translated by Takashi Kodaira and Alfred Marks.

summer's morning:
a child of the poor
drags a head of cabbage

IPPEKIRO NAKATSUKA

She had the most peaceful face. I would go to the Art Insti-
tute of Chicago to stare at the almost life-size carving of the
Sung Dynasty Chinese goddess Kwan Yin: sitting in medita-
tive repose on a lotus seat, head tilted, holding a flower, with
an air of calm. Her presence of compassion has stayed with
me all these years. Her name means "one who hears the suf-
fering cries of the world"; sometimes she is depicted with a
thousand arms to help many beings. In Asian cultures she
(though sometimes male or androgynous) is a bodhisattva,
one who gives up personal enlightenment to help all others.
This help, however, does not mean "idiot compassion" and
may involve "ruthless compassion," as Trungpa Rinpoche

said; for genuine compassion starts with clear seeing and openness and takes practice. Pema Chödrön, the Tibetan Buddhist meditation teacher, espouses the practice of alleviating suffering by changing our thinking little by little, by simply practicing *maitri* (loving-kindness) and breathing out the thought that others have well-being. A more challenging practice is tonglen (taking and sending), a practice which adds the dimension of thinking of taking in the suffering (of oneself and others) on the in-breath and breathing out well-being (for oneself and others) on the out-breath. Pema says, "Tonglen practice is a method for connecting with suffering—our own and that around us . . . a method for overcoming our fear of suffering . . . and a method for awakening the compassion inherent in all of us."[24] As in this haiku, simply breathing in the struggle of a child in poverty, and breathing out good wishes, as Kwan Yin.

IPPEKIRO NAKATSUKA (1887–1946). One of the great and truly modern Japanese haiku poets. A student of Hekigodo, he advocated free-verse haiku: often longer, without a 5-7-5 count or a kigo (season word). Yet he maintained Basho's humanism. Nakatsuka was editor of two modernist haiku magazines: *Kaiko* and *Etude*. His main haiku collection is *1,000 Haiku of Ippekiro*. Later collections are *Pomegranates* and *Cape Jasmine*.

calmly

he gazes at the mountain—

the frog

ISSA KOBAYASHI

It has taken a long time for "civilized" people to see beings of the animal realm as worthy of respect; to protect animal rights along with human rights. This is largely due to the Judeo-Christian commandment, "thou shall not kill," being reserved for humans and not animals, whereas other spiritual traditions, including the Buddhist and indigenous peoples such as the Native Americans, revere animals and all sentient beings as worthy of respect, and even as teachers or wise elders. The smallest to the largest—the ant, the frog, the crow, the bear—can be totems from whom we can learn the wisdom of work, play, attention, and strength. And love—who has not felt this from our cat or dog? Animals initially provided guidance to the first humans who emerged on the earth; humans learned how to survive by observing their animal teachers, who were here first. Even the flickering bison on the caves of Lascaux reflect a mystical interdependency of all beings and an awe of life's intertwining of birth and death; hunting was done with a prayerful attitude of gratitude. To honor the wisdom of animals and all sentient beings is to see them as equals in a world, which we do not dominate but rather share, and thus recognize and keep the fragile biodiversity of all creatures on our planet. This haiku reflects the poet's Shinto and Buddhist roots of seeing other creatures as worthy of respect as much as humans: so here the frog is also conscious and enjoys the mountain view, of perhaps even Mount Fuji or Mount Everest.

ISSA KOBAYASHI (1763–1828). One of the three greatest traditional Japanese male haiku poets, along with Basho and Buson. As a Pure Land Buddhist, he espoused compassion for all living things, perhaps because he himself had a life of poverty and personal tragedy. See his autobiographical haibun collection, *Oraga Haru* (The Spring of My Life) from 1819.

along with spring leaves
my child's teeth
are coming in

KUSATAO NAKAMURA

Happiness . . . that elusive state of being: the innate desire of all human beings and the yearning of all sentient beings, without exception, down to a child or tiny green leaf. It is the common thread that binds us all: wanting not to suffer but to be happy. In an age when there is so much suffering in the world, and we are inundated with this information, it seems overwhelming, almost hopeless; yet at the same time, it is urging us to feel this thread of connection more than ever. Because we cannot ignore it, we are left wondering: how can we be happy, much less consider and foster others' happiness? A quote by Shantideva, an eighth-century Indian Buddhist master, taken from his famous teaching the *Bodhi-*

charyavatara (the "Way of the Bodhisattva"), explains *how:* "If you want to be happy think of others / If you want to be unhappy think of oneself." At first it seems an odd reversal, but when tried, it is always true, for our own happiness is totally intertwined with others. As in this haiku, the happiness of the father comes out of his concerned thinking about his child growing and not wanting him to be in pain. A simple way to practice this is with a short Buddhist prayer, "The Four Limitless Ones," which is actually a universal compassion practice anyone can do, whatever one's belief or wherever one is—whether meditating and breathing out this thought or just sitting in a café: "May I, and may all beings, be happy and at peace and free from suffering." In this case, the father would extend his thinking to include all children. With this simple thought, the seed has been planted for happiness for oneself and other.

KUSATAO NAKAMURA (1901–1983). A prominent modern Japanese haiku poet. He first studied German literature, and then Japanese, especially the haiku poet Shiki. Nakamura was later a professor at Seikei Gakuen in Tokyo. He founded and led the Banryoku (Myraid Green Leaves) haiku group. Also, unlike most Japanese, he became a Christian. His works include *The Eldest Son, Volcanic Island,* and *Beautiful Farm.*

i catch
the maple leaf   then let
it go

JOHN WILLS

Holding and letting go: the distillation of life's path. In Buddhism the way to end suffering is to be nonattached. This seemed abstract to me until Mitsuo Aoki, a professor of religion at the University of Hawaii, whom I assisted years ago, kindly guided me through basic exercises he used in his "death and dying" and hospice center classes to "let go" of a lingering attachment to an ended relationship. It involved imagining that specific person in a chair and me saying unfinished words and good-byes, as well as physical exercises of tightening and relaxing my body. Although it wasn't an instant cure, I was no longer as fixated, for my mind and body had a glimpse of what "letting go" was, with the feeling of release and relief. I had glimpsed the importance of non-attachment. For it is not the thing itself—be it a relationship, a new car, or particular view such as patriotism—that is the problem; but it is our clinging to the thing even when it causes us, ourselves, and others mental or physical pain, which blinds us to a bigger view and snowballs into more suffering. Ultimately, the challenge of letting go becomes a spiritual act in some way: in many spiritual traditions, surrender is the backbone, as Mohammed says in the Qur'an, "True religion is surrender."[25] And so as we grasp at the beautiful red leaf, we just might let it spin again in the autumn wind, delighting in that tiny leaf-filled and empty moment.

JOHN WILLS (1921–1993). One of the earliest and prominent American haiku poets. Best known as a "naturalist" haiku poet from his experience of living on a farm for some years in the mountains of Tennessee with his wife, haiku poet Marlene Mountain. He was also a college teacher of literature. His works include *Weathervanes, Back Country, Cornstubble, Reed Shadows,* and his last collection, *mountain.*

A page of Shelley
brightens and dims
with passing clouds

ROD WILLMOT

"Oh wild West Wind, thou breath of Autumn's being . . ." It
blows the passing clouds and the sunlight comes and goes,
and time passes. Yet the eternal moment of time exists in the
mingling of various historic times in the kaleidoscope of this
very page: the page of Percy Shelley's paper as he scratches
out his poem in ink about two hundred years ago; the book
page of the haiku poet Rod Willmot some years ago read-
ing Shelley's poem "Ode to the West Wind" in sunlight, and
then recording his haiku response on another paper; the
page of paper or virtual screen that I am typing my meander-
ing thoughts on in 2007 in response to all of these; and the
page of this book that you, the reader, are hopefully distilling

some years later. Besides these five page-layers of time there is ultimately the page of blankness, of white space, which cradles us all in collective memory beyond the breath of time— a place where all of these pages seen at different times co-emerge and remain this very moment again and again. Our breath rises and falls together with the wind: "The trumpet of a prophecy! O, Wind, / If Winter comes, can Spring be far behind?"[26]

ROD WILLMOT (b. 1948). One of the foremost Canadian haiku poets. His best-known collections are *Haiku* and *Sayings from the Invisible*.

shaking
the packet of seeds
asking, *are you still alive?*

KIYOKO TOKUTOMI

In these uncertain times I find myself doing something I've never done before: I've started saving seeds. Seeds from apples and oranges or larger pit seeds from apricots and dates—whatever is in season. I now have jars of seeds—a mini version of the Global Seed Vault in Norway—I am saving for a future time, perhaps when food is scarce and resources limited. My logical mind says "foolish" but something deep within makes me do it. Although I have worked as a gardener, I don't have a garden right now. Whether I eventually use and plant the seeds is not the point. It is just symbolic of the human yearning to keep a connection to Nature, to reaffirm the fragile sacredness of life: to simply plant a seed and watch it grow into green—renewal and trust in Nature, with the urge to protect these sacred seeds. It's also symbolic of trust in the future, that the seeds of life remain, for Nature is wiser and will outlast us. The life force of seeds is unstoppable. Like the story of Japanese-Americans interned in camps in Tule Lake, in Northern California, during World War II; the only thing that sustained their hope was the writing of haiku and the saving of seeds, one of the few possessions they could carry with them and keep.[27] Likewise, this above haiku shows the warm respect the poet has in talking to the tiny sentient seed beings with trust that they are still alive and will grow no matter what we larger sentient beings deem to do on this planet, in times of war or peace.

KIYOKO TOKUTOMI (1928–2003). A prominent Japanese-American haiku poet and haiku teacher. She was born in Japan but lived most of her adult life in Southern California with her husband, the late haiku master Kiyoshi. Together they created the active American haiku group, the Yuki Teikei Haiku Society (based in California), which adheres to the traditional 5-7-5 syllable count for English haiku. Her bilingual collection is *Kiyoko's Sky: The Haiku of Kiyoko Tokutomi,* translated by Patricia J. Machmiller and Fay Aoyagi.

when the spade turns
the soil in our garden—
how different . . .

ION CODRESCU

Yes, the smell of the earth after a rainstorm. As in this haiku
we can smell and remember the earth, the turned-over soil,
under our feet, taken for granted. It awakens something deep
within us. Modern biologists, inspired by James Lovelock
and others, have posed the possibility that our earth is Gaia
(the Greek goddess of the Earth) our Mother, as in most in-
digenous peoples' beliefs, and is actually a living organism
with a consciousness. And all sentient beings, including we
humans, may be her cells and neurons, as in the microcosm of
our own body and mind consciousness. From the subatomic
to the galactic, there are interactions taking place not just on
the earth but between our earth's electromagnetic body and

the galaxy and multiverses. At first it seems a strange hypothesis, but something within us feels its possible truth. And as ecologically conscious beings beyond an anthropocentric worldview, we no longer see the earth as a simple spherical mass that we can exploit for our benefit, culminating in the destruction of the earth's ecosystems: global warming, deforestation, desertification, water scarcity, air and water pollution, and the loss of species. Chief Seattle reminds us of the reality of our interrelated cosmos espoused by his Native American tradition, as well as modern physics, Buddhism, and sustainable environments. "The earth does not belong to us. We belong to the earth. All things are connected like the blood that unites us all. Humans did not weave the web of life; we are merely a strand in it. Whatever we do to the web, we do to ourselves."[28] Breathing in the fresh scent of the earth we remember, "Gaia, Gaia, Gaia, we are all the breath of Gaia!"[29]

ION CODRESCU (b. 1951). A prominent Romanian haiku and renku poet. In the 1990s he founded the Constantza Haiku Society. He is the creator and editor of *Hermitage: Haiku Journal,* an international journal. Among his poetry books are *Drawings among Haiku, A Forest Guest,* and *Mountain Voices.*

> ancient pond—
> frog jumps in
> sound of the water

BASHO MATSUO

Our blue planet, an iridescent pearl hanging in dark space—
blue because of water. However, only 3 percent of the world's
water is fresh and only 1 percent accessible to more than
6 billion humans and other living creatures. Water, the most
essential, yet taken-for-granted element: no living creature
can live without it. Since the Ice Age, water levels have been
constant, until human pollution of ground water, destruc-
tion of rivers, lakes, and wetlands, soil erosion, and so on, left
us in crisis. More than 1 billion people lack adequate water,
and by 2030 that number could be half the world's people,
creating "water wars." Those in affluent countries consum-
ing a hundred gallons a day, instead of the minimum five

to fifteen gallons, must reconsider humanity. I remember India's countryside: women in saris swaying, walking many miles, carrying clay jugs of water on their heads. While others like myself, fortunate to be living near freshwater Lake Michigan, can hear the water against the shore and water from the tap; yet I know it is tenuous even here, with the threat of industrial dumping. Yet wherever our water comes from, we can be grateful for this life source: conserve it, protect it, and share it. For we are essentially water: born in water and remain 70 percent water. The Japanese scientist Masaru Emoto talks about water crystals having conscious energy, which responds to positive human thoughts, and enhances the circulation of water in our bodies and on our planet.[30] We need to remember we are water drops in *one* pond; otherwise Basho's famous frog will have no pond to jump into and there will be no sound of water.

BASHO MATSUO (1644–1694). The greatest haiku poet in Japanese history. Coming from a low samurai class, he later became a renga master with many disciples, studied Zen, and traveled widely. He took haiku to a deeper level, espousing haikai no michi (the Way of Haiku) as a way of life and a return to Nature. See *Sarumino* (*Monkey's Raincoat*, a renga collection); and *Oku no Hosomichi* (*Narrow Road to the Interior*, a haibun collection). See also haiku translations in R. H. Blyth's *History of Haiku,* vol. 1 and Makoto Ueda's translation *Basho and His Interpreters*—just some among many translations.

After weeks of watching the roof leak
I fixed it tonight
by moving a single board

GARY SNYDER

Harmony: the idea is not so much to live in harmony with Nature as it is to live in the grace of *wild nature,* as epitomized by the poet Gary Snyder following the footsteps of Thoreau, Taoist mountain hermits, and Buddhist teachers. *Wild* here refers to nature in process with little or no human intervention: a holistic ecology of "going with" Nature rather than "going against" Nature. As he has said, "We need a civilization that can live fully and creatively together with wildness."[31] This Way of Harmony would include the Hindu-Buddhist concept of *ahimsa,* of causing the least possible harm to anything in Nature, stemming from the idea of interdependency. And it would also include the idea from Taoism, that if left to its natural course, things in Nature will eventually come to a point of balance. This view, which is something for us to contemplate, is reflected simply, almost humorously, through this rare haiku from Snyder's *Hitch Haiku* series. It is rare because, even though Snyder introduced early translations of haiku to his Beat poet friends, studied Eastern philosophy, lived some years in Japan, and practiced Zen Buddhism, over the years his focus has mostly been on imagist poems and essays on Nature and ecology, rather than haiku. Yet all of his poems reflect a haiku sensibility with haiku images embedded throughout. But more important, the haiku spirit of Basho's edict, "Return to Nature, follow Nature…"[32] is found in the breath of his words, in a single board.

GARY SNYDER (b. 1930). America's foremost Nature poet of our time, as well as a Nature essayist. He is the author of many books, including the poetry collections *Turtle Island, The Back Country, Axe Handles,* and *Mountains and Rivers Without End.* His collections of essays include *The Real Work, The Practice of the Wild,* and *Back on the Fire.* He has also translated the Chinese poet Han Shan in *Riprap and Cold Mountain Poems.* Among his awards are the Pulitzer Prize (1975), the Bollingen Poetry Prize, and the Japanese Masaoka Shiki International Haiku Prize (2004). He's lived close to wilderness his whole life with his family, and in the Sierra Nevada foothills since 1970.

a white lotus—
the monk decides
to cut it!

BUSON YOSA

Cut! The monk hesitates—and then decides to cut the flow-
er, while knowing how every action has consequences under
the law of karma. The karmic cut is heightened because the
lotus is a Buddhist symbol of potential enlightenment, for
the pure flower grows out of muddy water. *Karma* is the San-
skrit word for "action": whatever we do or even think now,
plants a seed that will grow to fruition in the future. Actually
many causes and conditions must coemerge for something
to happen. Every cause becomes an effect and every effect
another cause, for all is intertwined in the tapestry of karma.
The monk's cutting the flower could lead to various effects,
depending upon the intent and situation. Perhaps he cut it

as a "crazy wisdom act" to show his spontaneous enlight-
enment, but the head monk thought it was egoistic and hit
him; perhaps he cut it for the holiday shrine and the flower's
beauty was appreciated by all; perhaps he cut it for a lovely
nun at a nearby temple, but the monastery found out and
dismissed him, creating further disharmony, for the monk
was the temple gardener . . . On goes the wheel of karma; no
one is exempt. Since every action creates positive or negative
karma, our intention is most important; so we need to pause
and ask ourselves if this action will not only benefit me, but
benefit others as well. To pause and care about decisions, not
out of fear but out of respect for karma. For as Dilgo Khyen-
tse Rinpoche, the twentieth-century meditation master, sur-
prisingly said in a lecture once, "karma is more exact than a
bank account." That is surely something to pause over when
holding the scissors before the white lotus.

BUSON YOSA (1716–1784). One of the three greatest male haiku and
renga poets (along with Basho and Issa), Buson was also a great painter
of the literati art style and a master of vividly elegant images, which are
evident in his haiku. He also illustrated Basho's haiku. Born in Osaka,
he was at first a student of Kikaku, a close disciple of Basho. He later
promoted the "back-to-Basho revival" that restored haiku to its former
state. Some works include *Ake Garasu* (A Crow at Dawn) and *Shin
Hanatsumi* (New Flower Picking).

a stick goes over the falls at sunset

COR VAN DEN HEUVEL

A warm autumn day. The sunlight warm on my face and shoulders. Basking. The light comes and goes . . . the light not here, then here, and then gone. I am not here. Now I am here. And then not here again. The cycle of life. As we watch a stick going over the falls in fading sunlight. So what, so ordinary. But what a *so,* a *so* filled with wonder, it is extraordinary. As the Zen masters say, the "just so" of things as they are, the big *it,* is all there really is, where the ordinary and extraordinary are *one.* As in this ritual: the Hawaiian hula dancer throws a white flower *lai* into the volcano in prayer to the goddess Pele; the ritual seems extraordinary, but on another level it is ordinary: a plant thrown into a pit. Just as the ordinary stick becomes extraordinary in the sunlight in our lucid perception. All depends upon our perception: of being totally present, of having the doors of perception cleansed a la William Blake. This present moment is the seed of wonder that grows the more we attend to it. And even if all the world's libraries (of paper and cyber books) were destroyed, like the Alexandria Library eons ago, something would remain because human beings possess this sense of wonder we can always tap into. So we watch the stick go. And then we, too, go. Yet the wonder remains for the next stick at sunset. The next open eye to perceive the grace of luminosity.

COR VAN DEN HEUVEL (b. 1931). A prominent American haiku poet and promoter of haiku. He is best known for editing collections of American and Canadian haiku, including *The Haiku Anthology: Haiku and Senyru in English* and *Baseball Haiku: The Best Haiku Ever Written About the Game*. His own haiku books include *Dark* and *Puddles*. He is also the author of the controversial one-word haiku: "tundra." He is also the winner of the Masaoka Shiki International Haiku Prize and past president of the Haiku Society of America.

a warm fall day,
learning from this rock
to do nothing

PAUL O. WILLIAMS

Learning from Nature: from the sky openness, from the earth change and renewal, from this rock stillness. How difficult for most postmodern people to "do nothing," to just be with ourselves without distractions, entertainment, or time constraints, to get beyond feeling it is a waste of time or even a sin. How different from native peoples or our ancient ancestors more than ten thousand years ago, who could "just be," sitting around the fire; when not hunting, gathering, or sleeping, there was the storytelling, singing, and dancing around the fire—and then the long intervals of just sitting and being, watching the embers of the fire. Actually the most contentment I've ever felt was years ago visiting the Karen hill-tribe peoples of northern Thailand, and staying overnight at the women's lodge: a simple, open, thatched hut on stilts, where after dark the women, young and old, gathered around the fire pit. The older women sat up and smoked their long pipes and the younger women reclined on their mats as I did. Not a word was spoken for hours, for the whole night . . . everyone stared into the fire that was illuminating the darkness. It was primordial: it was silent and it was harmonious. It was "doing nothing," yet it was "doing something" in the sense of being fulfilled and complete—nothing was missing, all was perfect as it is. Verse 37 of the *Tao Te Ching* reminds us of the concept of *wu-wei* (nonaction): "The Tao takes no action and yet there is nothing left undone."[33] Then the space opens up for myriad possibilities to take place. The rock becomes our teacher: be like the mountain, just sitting still.

PAUL O. WILLIAMS (b. 1950). A well-known American haiku poet who is also a science-fiction writer. He served as president of the Haiku Society of America. His many poetry books include *The Edge of the Woods*. He was editor of *The Gulf Within: 1992 Gulf War Poems*.

The time it takes—
for snowflakes to whiten
the distant pines.

LORRAINE ELLIS HARR

The whiteness of snow: the unknown, the blankness, the uncertainty of white space. And the waiting interlude. Yet in this haiku there is almost no waiting, no time—it seems beyond time. How much easier it seems, to watch snow whiten the landscape, than to wait in stalled traffic, in a hospital bed, or for a delayed friend in a café. Nature is beyond our overlay of human time. Perhaps that is the key to patience: letting go of expectations, letting things evolve more naturally and grow in their own time, in their "natural" time; all things, including us, being of and from Nature. Somehow we have forgotten this and have become disconnected from the natural rhythms of life: the rhythm of the rise and fall of each moment, to be aware in the present, breath by breath. For if we could be attentive to this very moment, our mind could relax more, and we would not be as bored or impatient, but be with whatever is happening: watching the fumes rise from the cars in front of us, watching the IV drip through the tube, watching the shadow move across the coffee cup—or just watching snow whiten the pines, snowflake by snowflake, as if the snow is breathing with us, with each breath.

LORRAINE ELLIS HARR (1912–2006); pen name Tombo (dragonfly). One of the prominent and active early American haiku poets. Her works include *Snowflakes in the Wind*, *Cats Crows Frogs & Scarecrows*, and *Seventy-Sevens: Pathways of the Dragonfly*.

across the fields of stubble
flame   stalks   flame

DAVID COBB

The primordial energy of fire, most powerful, awesome of the four elements, expressed in this two-line haiku's stalking flame. The stars'—and especially our sun's—power gives heat, light, and fertility for life. In many cultures' creation myths, or origin-of-fire myths—like the sun god Ra of Egypt or the sun goddess Amaterasu, of Japan—the sun is the cradle of life. Our relationship to fire is gratitude on the one hand, and fear and awe on the other. Sunrise. The flash of fireflies. Turner's luminous skies. A lamp in the dark. Heat lightning over the Serengeti. The fire pits of Neanderthals. The neon signs of Ginza. An earthquake's molten fires. Lovers embraced in Vesuvius's ash. Copernicus burned at the stake. Raging forest fires. Sunlit grapes pressed into wine. The flash of Nagasaki's mushroom cloud. Lit-up city lights seen from space stations above Earth. Mothers stirring soup over hot fires for millennia. And electricity's pulse, a belt of chromosomes strung around the Earth . . . We are born of a spark of this energy from sperm and egg, and after we die we are cremated or go back into particles through earth's organic heat. From fire to ash to fire again: the phoenix, that is fire. And in between the fire's incarnations, we can still enjoy the heat of the sun on our back and the starry night's light beckoning overhead—for we know we are both the dust of the stars and the fire of the stars.

DAVID COBB (b. 1926). Prominent and active British haiku poet. He was a founding member and president of the British Haiku Society. His poetry collections include *A Leap of Light, Jumping from Kiyomizu,* and *Mounting Shadows.* His books on haiku include *The Genius of Haiku: Readings from R. H. Blyth, Japanese Haiku: British Museum Haiku,* and *Haiku and the Poetry of Nature.* He was coeditor of the *Iron Book of British Haiku.*

the wind
forced to blow
on concrete, steel, and glass

JACK CAIN

The power of wind: air, the last of the four elements. The breath of life we take in every moment, so elemental we barely realize it until it is gone, until a breeze cools us or until a windstorm rattles the house. In many native cultures, the wind is the life force, external and internal. In Tibet the mountaintops are filled with colorful *lungta* (windhorse) prayer flags, which carry peaceful wishes on sacred wind energy. In the Japanese tradition, the *kaze* is wind, and the *kamikaze* (unlike the "suicide bombers" in World War II), in its original Shinto meaning, is the "divine wind" imbuing each thing. In the Greco-Roman tradition, the *spiritus* is the breath of life within each living thing as well. There is also subtle vibratory wind energy, circulating within the body as well as the mind, that Indians refer to as *prana*, Chinese as *chi*, Japanese as *ki*, Tibetans as *lung*, and Navajos as *nichi'i*. All living things have this internal energy; even modern physics says all of space—from the vast to the subatomic—consists of multiverses and multidimensions of this vibrating energy. So in our postmodern culture, we must respect this life force: nurture it internally by raising our own mind-body energy, and protect it externally by stopping further pollution due to human over-industrialization, deforestation, and pesticides—harming bees, for example, who pollinate the plants and trees that purify our air. We must always use this sustainable wind energy, like solar energy, to keep the planet green. The above "city haiku" is looking at Nature from the wind's point of view instead of the human. Yet eventually, the concrete, glass, and steel will be dust blowing in the sacred wind, becoming part of it, again.

JACK CAIN (b. 1940). One of the foremost and active Canadian haiku poets, known for his controversial haiku, "an empty elevator / opens / closes." He is well published in prominent haiku magazines.

moonlight—
    a sand dune
    shifts

VIRGINIA BRADY YOUNG

Ultimately what is most remembered of civilizations is not the glory of war but art; after the dust settles, remnants of art remain. And even if all art were lost, the creative potential of art always remains within human beings. In most cultures, the artist acts as a shape-shifter or shaman, for true art involves sacred activity. Modern society seems to have forgotten this potent power of art: something that alters us, that makes us shift. We shift into a state of perplexity in front of a splashed Pollock painting or shift into a state of awe in front of Michelangelo's *David,* depending upon our personal likes and dislikes. Yet something occurs almost imperceptibly, no matter what—the best art being a journey of discovery, a reunion with something known before, getting to that place within us that points to the creative mystery inside each and every living thing. A child draws her first circle and there is recognition ... and the Zen master draws a circle and there is another recognition. This haiku, in five little words, perfectly reflects such a shift into the intuitive mode under moonlight, in less than one breath.

VIRGINIA BRADY YOUNG (b. 1918). One of the earliest foremost American haiku poets. She studied poetry with Robert Frost and Anne Sexton and, at the request of William Stafford, recorded her poems for the permanent collection of the Library of Congress. She is a past president of the Haiku Society of America. Her main works include *warming a snowflake, Shedding the River,* and *Circle of Thaw.*

the piercing cold—
in our bedroom stepping
on my dead wife's comb

BUSON YOSA

This haiku has been criticized for being too subjective and emotional, but that is why people like it. Even though Buson supposedly wrote it years before his wife died, it poignantly depicts the courage needed even to admit this kind of painful experience. All of us inevitably experience fear: fear of loss, of death, of pain, of failure, or being alone, poor, unloved . . . And we pray for the courage to face it: not to hide from it or grit our teeth, but rather, as is taught in Tantric Buddhism, "to lean into the painful points" as a way to acknowledge and transmute it. For once we are able to face our pain, no matter how long it takes, our heart cracks open, like "the piercing cold" of autumn's chill intensified by stepping on something sharp under our foot that hurts us physically—and in this case, in a traditional Japanese house, Buson would have been walking barefoot on straw tatami mats, so it would have been extremely piercing. But it would hurt us even more emotionally to touch a loved one's personal lacquer comb and feel all the memories attached to it. This is the fearless moment: when we can keep awareness on the pain, somehow the fear lessens and our heart softens, which is the seed for compassion for ourself and others. Even if we can do this for only a fleeting moment; we have been fearless: we have faced pain, the bite of death. This is the way of courage: to live fully by being open to all of life, both its joy and its pain. The comb reminds us.

BUSON YOSA (1716–1784). One of the three greatest male haiku and renga poets (along with Basho and Issa), Buson was also a great painter of the literati art style and a master of vividly elegant images, which are evident in his haiku. He also illustrated Basho's haiku. Born in Osaka, he was at first a student of Kikaku, a close disciple of Basho. He later promoted the "back-to-Basho revival" that restored haiku to its former state. Some works include *Ake Garasu* (A Crow at Dawn) and *Shin Hanatsumi* (New Flower Picking).

the spirit, the truth
of silent prayer—
just the moon on the road

KIKUSHA-NI

Perhaps every haiku is a silent prayer in the broader sense. The medieval German Christian mystic Meister Eckhart said that if the only prayer we used in our life was "thank you," that would be enough; and no matter what our situation, even if lying sick or dying in bed, we can still say "thank you" and perhaps even pray for others' well-being. Eckhart also said that "the eye with which I see God is the same eye with which God sees me,"[34] a view which is quite compatible with haiku's spirit of being one with Nature. For each haiku is a grateful acknowledgment of the sacred, rather an honoring of the sacred in each and every thing: each caw of a crow, each dewdrop on a leaf, each child's scream, each empty street. Whether good, bad, happy, or sad, we honor it, as part of the spirit and truth we call "life." In this haiku the focus is on the moon, which represents the truth of sacredness, silent prayer, and the symbol of enlightenment to awaken us. This awakening is epitomized in this other, rare haiku of writer-metaphysician Susan Edwards, "the moon / from behind the cloud / awakens the sleepy meditator."[35] This is the role of haiku, as prayers to awaken us, like the faint smoky notes of a Korean *piri* flute, heard from another valley on a hazy moonlit night.

KIKUSHA-NI (1752–1826); her family name was Tagami. One of the best known of the traditional Japanese women haiku poets. A student of haiku poet Sankyo, she was also proficient in the arts of calligraphy, painting, Chinese verse, and *waka* (court poetry). After her husband died she became a Buddhist nun at twenty-four and she made a pilgrimage all over Japan for thirty years as a carefree spirit. Her verse is collected in *Taorigiku* (Plucked Mums). This haiku was written for her Buddhist teacher.

my birthday—
yellow dust blows in
from China

MASAHISA FUKUDA

All of life has its cycles: the seasonal change from hot to cold,
wet to dry—one day we are swimming in the lake and the
next day a red leaf blows across our path and we know it's
another season. Just as in this haiku, the poet notes his birth-
day has arrived, but instead of seeing it solely in the micro-
cosm of his personal life—that the yellow dust will make it
unpleasant for his celebration—he sees it in the macrocosm
of vaster Nature. This view seems humble, that the human
rituals we put so much stock into pale in the light of Nature's
cycles. This perspective makes birthdays not separate, but
a part of Nature's yearly spring phenomenon of yellow dust
blowing in from China to Japan. The cycles of our lives are

part of a much greater cycle than we can ever fathom. Human rituals are so important, but at the same time so ordinary. We need to mark them, in order to appreciate them, but at the same time we need to also see them as no big deal, as part of the greater cycle of the universe. If we could only see ourselves as both everything and nothing, as both gold and dust at the same time, perhaps as yellow dust.

MASAHISA FUKUDA (1935–2005); pen name was Shinku. One of the well-known Japanese haiku and renku (group linked verse) poets of modern times, as well as a Basho scholar. He was a promoter of international renku for "world peace," through the work of his group and magazine, *Amanogawa* (Milky Way), based on Sado Island in Japan. Among his works are *Chikyu Renku O Tamoshimou* (Let's Enjoy Renku Together), *Basho no Kokoro* (Heart of Basho), and his own haiku collection *Amanogawa*.

after the dancing—
the wind in the pines
and the insects' cries

SOGETSU-NI

Most spiritual traditions have a fool or trickster to provoke us into awakening; in Tibetan Buddhism there is the female *dakini* principle that provokes us, through peaceful or wrathful means, to awaken more fully into a lightness of being. These days we know little about true play, to enjoy letting go into our intuition and imagination. For some it is laughing with a glass of wine, skipping stones on the beach, or playing with a child or kitten. For most, from the Stone Age on, spontaneous singing and dancing was a natural pastime. And for some in the Islamic Sufi tradition, there are even the whirling dervishes who dance ecstatically in circles to commune with the Mystery. This haiku depicts nighttime dancing in the poet's neighborhood, in which everyone participates, during the Obon (spirit of the dead) summer festival. The human celebration is followed by Nature's celebration, which is a constant, once we stop and listen to the wind and insects. The great modern Korean poet Ko Un explains it well: "There is the word *p'ungnyu* in Korean, which expresses 'wind' and 'flow,' a kind of yin and yang. It's the dance that comes out of the union of humans and nature. It is the harmony of the human experience of nature—wind and flow—out of which music, dance, and poetry emerge. There's a spirit presence within that descends. . . . This concept has vanished from modern education. . . . It is related to Buddhism, Taoism, and shamanism."[36] The natural rhythms of the cocreating dance of humans and Nature.

SOGETSU-NI (d. 1804); her family name was Imaizumi. One of the better-known traditional Japanese women haiku poets. She was the wife of Tsunemaru, a main student of haiku master Shirao Kaya (1735–1792), who was a leader in the haiku world and taught the art of "unornamented haiku." She became a Buddhist nun in her later life.

how easily it glows
how easily it dims
the firefly . . .

CHINE-JO

Of all the words of my teacher, Trungpa Rinpoche, I remember these often repeated words the most: "Don't be afraid to be yourself, who you are."[37] Actually he was defining how we can be our own brave selves in the world. How much easier it seems for the firefly to brighten and extinguish, than for us to trust ourselves and be ourselves; of course, try as we might, ultimately we cannot do otherwise, so the joke is really on us. Being oneself is related to being relaxed with oneself and not embarrassed with oneself—a trust in our basic nature, which on the absolute level is as luminous as the light of the firefly; yet a luminosity that is sometimes dimmed by our own self-doubt, self-hatred, and confusion. The fire-

143

fly is following its nature of being a firefly, true to itself; and with inner courage and trust we can also do as Shakespeare's Hamlet was admonished to do: "to thine own self be true ..." In this particular haiku, since it is the poet's death haiku, she is reflecting on life's impermanence as well as how easily the firefly accepts its life and death and just being-ness in between: living gracefully, living true.

CHINE-JO (1660–1688). One of the leading woman poets of Basho's time. She was the younger sister of the haiku poet Kyorai, who was one of Basho's ten main disciples. In her twenties she wrote *renga*, with her older brother; these poems are recorded in her travel diary, *Ise Kiko*. Her verses were considered better than his. In fact, after her early death, Basho wrote a haiku for her: "summer airing / of wardrobes— / now also for the deceased."

cherry blossoms fallen—
people's hearts
serene again

KOYU-NI

Cherry blossoms, or *sakura,* are a cliché image of Japanese culture and a paradigm of exoticism, along with geisha and samurai, that is hard to bypass. However, traditionally they were the symbol for the samurai, for the flower's life only lasts a few days. I didn't understand its pervasiveness in Japanese art and poetry until I visited Japan in the spring. Walking along a long path lined with a canopy of cherry trees in full bloom, I was stunned by the beauty, as if William Blake's starry heavens had opened up: "To see a world in a grain of sand / And a heaven in a wildflower / Hold infinity in the palm of your hand / Eternity in an hour."[38] It was a slip into eternity, beyond human time and space, a moment of awe, things perfect as they are. In this very simple haiku, the poet depicts the aftermath of this cherry-viewing season when a Shinto-based culture reveres and delights in Nature, even in the midst of modern environmental ruin, and everyone comes out of their houses, day or night, to sing and dance—often drunk on sake—together under the blossoms in every inch of green across Japan, leaving the remains of the feast for the crows. After the excitement, there is the silence again, the calmness, the quiet faces on quiet trains. But for a moment, we are back to a primordial time of abandonment to pleasure, of being alive in Nature's renewal. In fact, this value of pleasure was codified in the Edo period as *ukiyo-e,* "the floating world" famously depicted in wood-block prints. Originally a Buddhist term for "this transitory life," it was later used to convey the seizing of the fleeting moment's sensual pleasures, without any guilt whatsoever. Ah, the pleasure of it!

KOYU-NI (d. 1782); her family name was Matsumoto. One of the more prominent woman poets of the Edo period. She learned haiku from Songi the First.

white frost—
the nun's worn wicker basket
starts the journey

SONO-JO

Throughout human history the theme of the journey or pilgrimage is found in most wisdom traditions, for example, the outward journey taken by Odysseus in search of his father, the Jews in search of a Promised Land, Buddha in search of the cause of suffering, King Arthur in search of the Holy Grail. Pilgrimages to sacred sites are a part of the human yearning for spiritual renewal: Catholics to Mexico City's Our Lady of Guadalupe, Jews to Jerusalem's Wailing Wall, and Muslims to Mecca's Kaaba. The outward journey becomes an inward journey, "the vision quest" for meaning and fulfillment, as in the Native American tradition. Joseph Campbell talks about how all the world mythologies of the "vision quest," especially of the mythic hero, have the same pattern: the descent into the unknown, the transformation or fulfillment, and then the return. Sometimes we purposely go on a quest and sometimes we are thrown into it; if we are fortunate, our consciousness is changed and we find our truth, which is a new way of being or giving birth—in fact, the mother giving birth is seen in this light as the original hero. We may not be heroic and save the world, but rather we save ourselves; yet this in turn vitalizes the world—if we can do as Campbell suggests, "follow our bliss,"[39] which is the path most natural for each of us. The Buddhist nun in this haiku is also on her spiritual journey to many temples, as was the custom of her day, even with its hardships of cold weather and walking on mountainous roads three hundred years ago by foot. We only need to place our foot down on the earth and take a step.

SONO-JO OR SONOME (1664–1726); her family name was Shiba. One of the most renowned traditional Japanese women haiku poets. Became Basho's student in 1689, and after his death in 1694 she studied with his foremost disciple, Kikaku. She worked as an eye doctor, haiku teacher, and haiku judge, and compiled haiku anthologies. She later became a Buddhist nun. Not long before Basho died he wrote this well-known haiku for her: "white chrysanthemum— / not a speck of dust / meets the eye."

the inner tide—
what moon does it follow?
I wait for a poem

DIANE DI PRIMA

The realm of creativity is interior, and is a mysterious interior journey. The Trappist monk Thomas Merton said, "our real journey in life is interior. . . ." To enter the realm of the interior, the moonlit night of dreams, of the Muse goddess, of howling she-wolves, we must leave behind boundaries, rules, and fixations and embrace the realm of intuition and imagination. Over her lifetime, the Beat poet Diane di Prima continues to rant, "the only war that matters is the war against the imagination." To protect and revere the imagination, we need to step beyond hope and fear and enter unknown territory. In Tibetan Buddhism this unknown is a *bardo,* or gap, the word often used for the place between death and rebirth—yet it is also a place of in-between states of our so-called awake life: a place of pregnant uncertainty and opening into creative space. Though mostly known for writing longer series of poems, di Prima has embraced haiku, and says about it: "Most recently it's been all about spaciousness, vastness in the fewest possible strokes. Images. Letting the breath open the sky."[40] And always, leaving the space for the moon to illuminate and move the tides.

DIANE DI PRIMA (b. 1934). One of the foremost American poets of the Beat literary renaissance, as well as a revolutionary activist, a Bohemian, a feminist, a poetry publisher, a teacher of poetry-alchemy-healing, and a practitioner of Zen and Tibetan Buddhism. She is also a cofounder of the San Francisco Institute of Magical and Healing Arts. Among her many published books are *Revolutionary Letters, Loba, Pieces of a Song,* a memoir titled *Recollections of My Life as a Woman,* and a haiku selection in the anthology *The Unswept Path: Contemporary American Haiku,* edited by John Brandi and Dennis Maloney.

closing the gate
alone with the stones
on this beautiful night

SHUOSHI MIZUHARA

The poet here has stepped beyond loneliness and embraced being alone in silence, in solitude. Most of our deepest moments occur when we are alone in silence or with others in silence. It is a gateway of nurturing, of healing, of renewal, and sometimes of revelation. The reverence for silence is in most religious traditions such as the Judeo-Christian statement, "Be still and know God," usually embodied in the Quakers' silent meetings. And it is often through solitude that we find the soft-heartedness to connect further to others. The poet here has also stepped into a communion with Nature, with the stones, on a moonlit night. Though we do not always regard them, stones are alive and have a spirit just as trees do. In Japan the Shinto custom of revering large rocks or trees by tying a rope around them marks a sacred space; the dry rock gardens of Zen temples such as Ryoan-ji quiet the mind; and *suiseki*—the Japanese word that refers to the East Asian art of using a stone placed on a wooden stand in the home to represent Nature's mountains—creates a calm ambiance. Across cultures, humans have been drawn to the sacredness of stones: sometimes huge stone sites such as Stonehenge of England or Uluru (Ayers Rock) of Australia; or small precious stones such as turquoise, amethyst, quartz crystal, or diamond; or even common stones we pick up on the beach. Lately I have gravitated to Petoskey stones, fossilized coral from 400 million years ago, found on Lake Michigan's beaches. These stones, as most stones in their quiet way, have healing energy. If we can be silent with stones, they just might be the greatest teachers of solitude.

SHUOSHI MIZUHARA (1892–1981). One of the great four S's of modern Japanese haiku poets. Following his father, he became a doctor, professor of medicine, and medical advisor for the Japanese Imperial Household. Initially a haiku poet of Kyoshi's Hototogisu (Cuckoo) group, he later formed his own group and magazine, *Ashibi* (Staggerbush), writing within the tradition yet colored with a dramatic sensibility. He is the author of more than twenty volumes of haiku, including *Verdure, Old Mirror, Loneliness on a Journey,* and *Martyrdom.*

ebb tide
sandpipers skitter
across her ashes

JERRY KILBRIDE

Ashes, of a name that cannot be named, in a place that is no place, in a time that is no time. Send them back. Send them back, ashes floating on water drops. The letters g-o-d carved on the bones, the smile of the flesh, the liquid reverberation of vocal cords, the sunlit glint of moving eyes—all back to ash, to Nature—and those alive go back to Nature as well for healing, for comfort, for understanding. With old age, sickness, and death, we turn to family and friends, but ultimately to Nature, from where we came and to where we return. We grieve . . . and then reflect. We find no absolute answer, but another paradox as we throw the ashes into the ocean . . . and they float back again to the shore as the sandpipers go about enjoying the waves, hunting for insects and snails, or chasing a mate, as they unknowingly trample over our loved one's ashes. It might make us cry even more, or perhaps laugh suddenly at this stark reality, yet it might also give us a moment of pausing, a healing moment of knowing that the eternal force we call this "life" continues in a mysterious way, as our breath, as wind rising and falling along with the waves, after the last breath.

JERRY KILBRIDE (1930–2005). A well-known American haiku poet and active member of the Haiku Society of America. Kilbride was a founding member of the Haiku Poets of Northern California and helped establish the American Haiku Archives in California. He was well published in haiku journals and his last collection was *Heaton Farm Haiku*.

autumn wind—
a hair has grown
on my mole

RYUNOSUKE AKUTAGAWA

Although this poet didn't live to be an old man, he insightfully sketched the aging process with a few words. It's almost too personal to speak about, almost ludicrous. As we face the mirror every morning and find another gray hair or mole, how do we react? Not many of us can see aging as life's process, as just another season. Not many of us can bypass the seductive ways of "staying young." Not many of us can age gracefully, without complaints of aches, without wishing for youth, without obsessing about wrinkles, without raging about lost freedom, and above all without regret. Caring for my parents now, I see both the difficulty and poignancy of aging and it makes me wonder if I will age gracefully or not.

Yet if we could accept aging, we could feel more contentment in our heart. Gratitude for what we have this very moment, no matter how fleeting, seems an essential key for contentment. Another key to aging gracefully would be relaxation through slowing down. I remember my Grandma Fries sitting quietly in her garden chair in summer and standing on her porch even in winter to bask in the sun. This ideal image of the old person, with serene face sitting on a porch in a rocking chair, seems almost impossible in our speedy youth-driven culture. Yet we could possibly let go into this natural rhythm of slowing down and find the grace of inner peace that naturally arises with appreciating what we have now: just sitting with the autumn sun and wind . . . and that could be enough.

RYUNOSUKE AKUTAGAWA (1892–1927). One of the foremost modern Japanese haiku poets, though mostly known as a novelist and short story writer. He was also a teacher of English and a translator of W. B. Yeats. Among his noted works are *Hell Screen, Kappa,* and, the most famous one, *Rashomon,* which was made into a memorable film by the director Akira Kurosawa. After a nervous breakdown, he died of an overdose of sleeping pills.

The sun glitters
on the path
of a snail

ROBERT AITKEN

This haiku was written the summer of 1944 in a Japanese internment camp for Americans in Kobe, Japan. The poet was a young civilian helping to build a submarine base on Guam when he was captured. As fate would have it, in the same prison camp, he met the British professor R. H. Blyth, a renowned translator of haiku, with whom he began studying haiku. After the war, and while studying with Japanese Zen masters, including Soen Nakagawa Roshi, who was also a haiku master, Aitken became one of the first American roshi (Zen master) in a Japanese lineage—and also a spokesperson for haiku in his books and *zendo* talks, which I feel grateful to have briefly attended. As a Buddhist teacher he uses haiku extensively. He often uses haiku to illustrate what he calls affinity or "the Tao of intimacy": it embraces karma, destiny, and synchronicity, but particularly the idea that everything is interconnected on such an intimate level that this moment's meeting or reading of this page came from an infinite network of perhaps lifetimes of preparation leading up to it, arising from an interplay with all beings, just as Aitken auspiciously found haiku. And through this intimacy, he said, "we are constantly being created and we are constantly creating others"[41] as in a dance. So in this haiku, the sun and the snail come together through the path, the path of intimacy, of stepping beyond the self: no sun, no snail, no path; only sun, snail, and path. Without separation, just a glint. The Buddha twirled a flower and the slime of the snail's path glittered.

ROBERT AITKEN (b. 1917). Aitken became one of the first American Zen masters in 1974, in the lineage of Hakuun Yasutani Roshi and Koun Yamada Roshi. He was also friends with the Zen scholar D.T. Suzuki. Aitken is the author of many books including *Taking the Path of Zen, Original Dwelling Place, Zen Wave: Basho's Haiku and Zen,* and *The Morning Star: New and Selected Zen Writings.* In 1959, with his wife Anne, he established the Diamond Sangha, a group of Zen centers. He still lives and teaches in Hawaii.

old posts and old wire
holding wild grape vines holding
old posts and old wire

ROBERT SPIESS

How did our postindustrial culture come to see daily work
as removed from spirituality, from the sacred? Some native
cultures still make clay pots with reverence and care and
put their breath of life into them. It's easy to forget that the
beautiful Hopi pots under museum glass were once used for
holding household water and were a part of everyday life.
This is not to now advocate forgoing our convenience of tap
and bottled water, but there has been a disconnect. Some of
this loss, reflected in boredom and detachment from work, is
the residue from industrialization's mass production, which
bypasses the individual's involvement; and also the remains
of the Western view of mind over body, which demeans

physical labor; though we find ourselves in another era, this postcolonial globalization still impacts our attitudes. However, some are now embracing a "spirituality of work," a primordial thread to the past beyond the "modern-postmodern work ethic" of just making money and a career track. In this approach, whatever work we choose to do, whether building fence posts, teaching children, or typing in an office, becomes a way to reconnect to the holiness of everything. When we reverently use our hands to recycle our cans and paper, when we thank our machines and tools for their good work for the day, when we think of greeting others at our workplace as the Hindus do, bowing with palms together, greeting the divinity within each of us, then and only then can we see any of our work—as the poet sees his old posts and wires as working along with Nature's grapevines—in a mutual cocreation of our work together on this earth.

ROBERT SPIESS (1921–2002). Important American haiku poet who shaped English-language haiku for half a century. He was the editor-publisher of the prominent haiku magazine *Modern Haiku* for twenty years. His collected works include *The Heron's Legs, Turtle's Ears, Five Caribbean Haibun,* and *Sticks and Pebbles.* He was also the winner of the Japanese Masaoka Shiki Haiku Prize. He loved canoeing his native streams of Wisconsin.

birthcry!
the stars
are all in place

RAYMOND ROSELIEP

The birthcry! We emerge from our greatest journey, from the dark womb into the light. And at the center is the Great Mother archetype; the creatrix goddess from whom all are born and thus become part of the cycle of birth, death, and rebirth. Regardless of our belief system, life involves transformation, yet not without pain and struggle. Whether visible or invisible, whether a physical birth or a spiritual birth, it is a transformation from one state to another: the fetus into the baby; the chrysalis into the butterfly; Orpheus's return from the underworld; the Egyptian god Osiris's resurrection; the ancient serpent shedding its old skin; Saint John of the Cross's "dark night of the soul"; Charles Dickens's Scrooge character reborn; Luke of the *Star Wars* films becoming a true warrior. For all the ancient mystery schools as well as modern paths, the evolution of consciousness is foremost: the death of the ego and the awakening of the soul or spirit into a higher consciousness. We can choose to take this journey or not; it is up to us. In the Buddhist view, a human birth is a precious opportunity, for it is purported to be the only realm affording the awareness to truth and enlightenment. For most people, it happens in tiny increments, as the Tibetan master His Holiness the Sixteenth Karmapa compassionately assured us in a talk, "Don't worry too much, though one isn't fully awakened this lifetime, one will eventually awaken, even if it takes hundreds or thousands of rebirths." And as this haiku points to the heavens, we are a part of the stars: we enter in perfection of the stars all in place, as in an astrology chart, and we take our DNA and our karma and the grace of awareness to practice just becoming a little bit kinder each day. That is our daily mystery school: simply following each moment's pregnant possibility of our birthcry into the light.

RAYMOND ROSELIEP (1917–1983). One of the foremost and most highly regarded pioneers of American haiku. Among his works are *Step on the Rain, Swish of a Cow Tail, Sailing Bones, Listen to Light,* and *The Earth We Swing On.*

I brush
my mother's hair
the sparks

PEGGY WILLIS LYLES

The intimacy of the everyday act of brushing hair. The spark, the fire . . . the torch from mother to daughter. Now the daughter brushes her mother's hair when she is old, yet the sparks remain . . . as the fire energy of the female, the goddess, the cradle of all life on this planet earth. The kiln fire tended by the women who shaped the first Paleolithic figures of the female form twenty-five thousand years ago; their buttocks, breasts, and pregnant bellies were prominent compared to their heads and limbs, yet the naked beauty of this pure form, seen in the most famous rounded fertility figure of the Venus of Willendorf. Likewise, in the Tibetan Buddhist tradition the feminine principle is called "the great mother" and is identified with transcendent wisdom (*Prajnaparamita*) and space, which gives birth to the phenomenal world. And as she gives birth and rekindles us, we can also remember to rekindle others—to rekindle those females suffering gender injustices, to keep their spark alive not only for their sake, but for the feminine principle existing within every human being, male or female alike. In the esoteric tantric tradition there is a female "flame-dancer dakini" (*dakini* means "sky-goer" and is the manifestation of the feminine energy principle in Tibetan Buddhism) who dances naked in flames, only clothed in the pure awareness of seeing all passions as energy waves of fire that she rides and emanates. The dakini's crimson body radiates the essence of perfect wisdom and the cosmic life force: blazing red flames spark from her body in the continual dance of birth, death, and rebirth contained in that eternal flame, to keep us aware of the sparks, within and without.

PEGGY WILLIS LYLES (b. 1939). One of the better known American haiku poets. Well published in haiku journals and contests, her best-known collected work is *Still at the Edge*.

reflected
in the sword's blade
soft summer clouds

GARRY GAY

Justice: the sword tempered in the fire, pounded thousands of times to produce strength. Yet the swordsman or swordswoman also needs to be tempered not just by hard steel training, but by the softness of clouds; to know the power of clouds is greater than the sword. For true justice, they must go hand in hand. Even Miyamoto Musashi, the greatest of all Japanese swordsmen, went from being a rebellious killer to a compassionate man of justice, after being captured and tempered for some years by a wise old monk in a mountain temple; the rest of his life was spent eradicating injustice wherever he found it. The compassionate heart makes us more aware of injustices everywhere; as the great civil rights minister and leader Martin Luther King Jr. said, "Injustice anywhere is a threat to justice everywhere."[42] The global injustices: the widening gap between rich and poor; the lack of women's rights to education, healthcare, sexual freedom, and economic independence; discrimination against people of homosexual and cross-gender orientation; and suppression and genocide of racial groups, not to mention religious groups. We can better honor the rights and inherent dignity of all oppressed people when we see the interconnection with the rights of people in our own families and communities, and vice versa. Yet compassion must be accompanied by wisdom and skillful means to carry it out. We need the modern woman warrior Rosa Parks, the black woman in Montgomery, Alabama, who sparked the civil rights movement in December 1955 by not taking injustice any longer—and she sat down at the front section of the city bus "reserved for whites only," just looking outside the window at the passing clouds.

GARRY GAY (b. 1951). Well-known American haiku poet from Northern California. Well-published in haiku magazines; some of his own collections are *Fig Newtons* and *Wings of Moonlight*. He is also an avid photographer.

shorter kisses
longer quarrels—
winter solstice

ERIC AMANN

I write this as we approach the winter solstice on December 21, the longest night of the year, when the days thereafter slowly become longer. Yet even though, since ancient times, people living in the northern hemisphere celebrate this slow return of the sun's light, the worse cold days are still many weeks away and it feels like a deeper wintertime. The cold and the darkness create a primordial feeling, a state of chaos on a cosmic scale out of which we originally emerged. As in this rather humorous haiku, it conveys how much human interaction is deeply interwoven with Nature's cycles; and that chaos is not problematic for Nature, but it often feels so to us humans. When this chaos happens on a global, national, family, or individual level, I try to remind myself of the Tibetan master Trungpa Rinpoche's memorable words, "Chaos should be regarded as very good news."[43] It doesn't always feel that way, but the chaos is a moment or time of lack of control and of surprise, in which anything is possible, beyond our judgment of good or bad. In Tibet it is believed that the enlightened Buddha energies manifest in either peaceful or wrathful forms, depending on what is called for, to protect and awaken us. The reason why it is "good news" is because the nonfixed, chaotic state of things creates an open field in which new things can emerge and grow: perhaps longer kisses or no kisses, perhaps even longer quarrels or no quarrels, or perhaps something entirely new and different—we never know.

ERIC AMANN (b. 1938). Although born in Germany, Amann is one of the leading Canadian haiku poets, besides being a critic and editor. He started the first Canadian haiku magazine, *Haiku,* in 1967. His collected work is *Cicada Voices: Selected Haiku of Eric Amann 1966–1979.*

first crickets—
the pulse
in my wrist

ADELE KENNY

The simple wisdom of our body: how it is a microcosm of the macrocosm of Nature, a reflection of the entire universe. If we could drop the conditioned notion in Western culture that the mind and body are split, we could embrace the interrelation of the mind-body as one whole gestalt. This unity includes the physical, mental, emotional, and spiritual realms. Even modern science and medicine admit the interdynamics of the mind and body: if one is sick, the other becomes sick, and if one is healthy the other becomes healthy. We would certainly be in better health, not so overweight or overwrought with stress-related mental and physical illnesses, if our mind and body were more harmonious. Health of the mind and body comes first from returning to a simple state of relaxation; the easiest for most is time-out, quiet, and deep breathing, even for a few minutes a day, which soon refreshes our mind and body. This also comes from simple attention to the body, as in the Zen saying: "When I'm hungry I eat; when I'm tired I sleep." This comes from being more sensitively attuned to our own bodies, feeling the beat of our heart and the pulse of our wrist. Most of all, this comes from feeling we are an integral part of Nature, with the crickets' rhythmic beats. Nature here is a reminder of our bodies, how both crickets and humans are singing together—the music of the spheres. A cricket beats and I beat; a cricket cries and I cry—not just in empathic symbiosis, but because ultimately we are not separate beings, with separate lives; we both breathe the same air under the same sky and the same stars, together.

ADELE KENNY (b. 1948). One of the more well-known American haiku poets. Kenny has been active in the haiku world and is a former president of the Haiku Society of America. Well published in haiku journals, her own works include *Castles and Dragons*.

terminally ill—
and her nails beautiful
by the wooden heater

DAKOTSU IIDA

The cabbages were planted in a row in front of the build-
ing in Seoul, just like Picasso's blooming flowers. At first it
stopped my mind, as another cultural sense of beauty, but
it was not a question of beautiful or ugly; it just was what it
was. Likewise, in our short life span, everything, including
our own body, is just what it is: in process of changing, which
includes the beautiful and the ugly, life and death. This haiku
poet's style, known for its austere beauty and quiet dignity,
gives us a raw, intimate portrait of this; it shows us the pri-
vate moment of caring for or visiting a dying loved one with
all the despair and degradation of the body's wasting away.
Yet in the midst of it, there is the gap of something else—in

that moment of Emily Dickinson's "a certain slant of light," with the heat warming the fingers, her nails become lustrous, beautiful. Some say an illness can be a journey, a chance for transformation, self-discovery; this is true for the ill person and true for those around her, if we have the courage to see what is there rather than what we want to be there: the stench of the sick room and lovely fingernails. It reminds me of a close friend's story of taking care of her mother in a hospice situation at home, and her mother wanting to make sure her fingernails were painted beautifully red, just so. It may seem superfluous or foolish to some, but in light of this haiku, it is just part of our journey of being with the way things are, as holy fools amid austere beauty.

DAKOTSU IIDA (1885–1962); pen name Sanro (Mountain Hut). A prominent Japanese haiku poet, considered a "modern Basho" because of his adherence to naked nature and a disciplined life. His haiku is likened to a large mossy rock in a mountain stream. Though he edited a local haiku magazine, *Isinglass,* he spent most of his life as a reclusive poet when not traveling in Korea and China. He lost most of his family in World War II. Among his works are *Collection of Poems at a Mountain Hut* and *Snowy Valley.*

> winter morning
> without leaf or flower
> the shape of the tree

L. A. DAVIDSON

Awakening in the morning and looking out the window fac-
ing the nakedness of winter: the stark beauty of Midwestern
winter trees. Thoughts drop away. In the white snowscape,
we see the shapes of things much differently, as if down to
their primordial design, down to each snowflake's crystal,
still visible to the eye. As if down to the shape of an angel's
wing, a white spider or white bone, it has our awestruck
attention. Yet without any snow whatsoever, as probably
meant in this haiku, the naked shape of the tree is even
clearer, as if black ink strokes were calligraphed against the
white space. Here the tree is seen in its "treeness," as if for
the first time, as if the incised Rosetta stone, which gave the

world the key to the ancient Egyptian script, suddenly clarifies what was lost before in eons of mist, and is now easily read and understood. This kind of epiphany cannot be artificially created—it is something that naturally unfolds when we come back to our open "beginner's mind" as the late Zen master Shunyru Suzuki always taught, and we can then begin to notice the shape of things around us. Ah! The potential for each moment to be an epiphany: for the outerscape and innerscape to merge and shape into a Rosetta stone, is always present.

L. A. (LAURA AGNES) DAVIDSON (1917–2007). "One of the most honored and respected American haiku poets. She exemplifies the poetic ideal of servitude to beauty and the truth," said the poet vincent tripi. When she was a child her family homesteaded in Montana. Later she lived with her husband in Uganda and Brazil. First introduced to haiku through the poet Elizabeth Lamb, Davidson promoted haiku for years and was vice president of the Haiku Society of America. Her works include *The Shape of the Tree* and *Bird Song More and More*.

> winter gusts—
> abortion herb has boiled
> and yet ...

SOJO HINO

In Japan, along winding alleyways in every neighborhood—
even in Tokyo—there is a tiny shrine to the "Jizo Bosatsu,"
a baby-"Buddha" stone statue (or sometimes rows of tiny
statues) usually clothed in a red apron with offerings of dolls
and toys around it: for it is to this compassionate image that
women come often to pray for their children who died young
or who were aborted. This poignant haiku deals with this
delicate, controversial subject, for it involves a deep moral
dilemma of a very personal matter. Some see ethics in a
cultural-social context as simply black and white, as Milton's
angels and Dante's devils, as a matter of right and wrong
moral laws to follow. Some see ethics in a situational context,

depending on the whole complex life situation, where shades of gray predominate. Some see ethics in a spiritual context, in which one's personal understanding and transformation are called for. It seems the bottom-line ethics of all wisdom traditions is to prevent suffering as much as possible: not to cause harm, or to cause as little as possible. In this case then, the most important question would be, "by this act, *whom* are we causing the most or least harm to": the mother, the father, the family, the unborn fetus, the community at large ... ? The question remains, almost like a Zen *koan*. Here the poet is witness to the pregnant woman's choice of her way of least harm in the act of abortion, and also witness to the pain of the human heart, no matter what is decided, contained in the words, "and yet ..."

SOJO HINO (1901–1956). One of the more outstanding of modern Japanese haiku poets. He spent his boyhood in Korea, where his father worked. He later worked as a manager for an insurance company while continuing to write haiku. He was also the editor of two haiku magazines, the seminal *Kikan* (Flagship) and later *Seigen*. He lost much in the air raids of World War II and was struck with lung disease and blindness; though bedridden for years, he still produced seven volumes of haiku over his lifetime.

full moon—
shadows of pines
on the straw mats

KIKAKU TAKARAI

Humans need beauty almost as much as bread; yet the beauty
of the everyday is often missed. In Japan, aesthetics have the
highest value. The bonsai tree and tiny high-tech camera or
robot share small size and elegant form to create a beauty of
simplicity taken from the *wabi-sabi* aesthetics of the art of
tea ceremony (begun in the fourteenth century): basically
sabi embodies a feeling of solitude, and *wabi* embodies a
weathered feeling of a small hut in the mountains or Van
Gogh's worn shoes. Some scholars say these aesthetics were
part of a Zen mystique used in the twentieth century to fit
into and also mystify Western culture; however, they still re-
flect some continuous indigenous values. For example, when

the first Japanese woman astronaut, Mukai Chiaki, went into the space shuttle, she spontaneously wrote the first part of a *tanka* poem and then asked the Japanese people, hooked up from far away on earth, to complete the poem; she received over 200,000 replies.[44] Of course, not all Japanese people like or write poetry, but a sense of beauty is valued. In fact, Japan was the only country to suggest putting a small room, modeled after a traditional tearoom, in the space station to create a quiet ambiance for meditation. The tearoom would include the natural beauty of tatami: the golden straw mats of traditional flooring, as in this haiku. Here, instead of being outside viewing the moon with the crowds, the poet is drinking sake in his room, enjoying the beauty of simplicity on his own floor.

KIKAKU TAKARAI (1661–1707). Perhaps the most famous of Basho's ten main male disciples. The son of a physician, Kikaku was talented in all the arts, but a wild rebel who loved sake and women as much as haiku. As a haiku teacher, he edited the haiku collections of Basho's school; the famous *Sarumino* (*Monkey's Raincoat*) is among them. This haiku is considered his masterpiece.

cherry tree watchmen
with their white heads
together

KYORAI MUKAI

Basho praised this haiku for having *sabishisa:* a loneli-
ness pervading all of life, nature as well as people. For even
though the old men are in stark contrast to the vibrant blos-
soms, they both have short lives: one has white hair and
one has three-day-long white petals. Yet we are all here to-
gether, in one shared community, as we work, as we play.
Here the old watchmen are workers, perhaps gardeners or
caretakers of cherry trees in a mountain community, temple
grounds, or nobleman's estate; perhaps they've worked to-
gether for years. Community is not something we create,
but something we need to recognize we are already in, inter-
dependently, and nurture it. There have always been local

communities of shared networks for survival, support, and comradeship, but much of this has diminished. Yet it seems that E. F. Schumacher's economic vision of "small is beautiful" is now becoming more of a necessity, calling for smaller communities, decentralization of corporate conglomerates, and using technology on a village scale. Fortunately, it is now becoming more of a reality with communities using the Internet, that is, if we know and trust our small community networks. This haiku conveys the poignancy of the transient communal life we deeply share: white heads together trimming the cherry trees or white heads together toasting over cups of sake! Here's to nurturing our small community, for it is a mirror of the vaster community of all people, all Nature.

KYORAI MUKAI (1651–1704). Perhaps the closest of Basho's ten male disciples. Kyorai was the son of a Confucianist, and a samurai adept in martial arts and astronomy. Rather than have many students, he was the disciple, along with Doho, to record Basho's poetic theories in *Haikai Mondo* in 1687, *Tabineron* (Travel Lodging Discussion) in 1699, and *Kyoraisho* (Kyorai's Gleanings) in 1704—all well used by haiku poets ever since.

beautiful lines
of green run through
the summer dishes

TATSUKO HOSHINO

This haiku is a good example of "kitchen haiku": written by women in a haiku world dominated by male poets in the early part of the twentieth century. It was a term used by male poets and critics to demean women's haiku as less important, for it was *only* about things "in the kitchen." Yet the kitchen is the most important place in the house, as the beating heart of the home and family. And here the lines of green Nature act as the umbilical cord. The green is the color of the vegetables of side dishes along with the rice and soup, and it is the color in the ceramics. The dishes make this a "home" and the "green" makes it an enlivened place. This haiku very simply conveys the feeling of home and family, of eating and being together. A place to share a life together; for as hard as that is for all of us, as social beings we mostly live in a family unit, whether one born into or one created. The "ideal home" has warmth, safety, relaxation, acceptance, and nurturance; a place to return to, where one can be oneself and feel at home. Yet in days of uncertainty—in the past, present, or future—many people are homeless or are war-torn refugees. If we are now fortunate enough to have a secure home, we can be grateful and pray for those who do not; most of all, we can remember that no matter what happens in this precarious life, the best refuge of home resides in our own heart and mind, to keep the ideal qualities of home within us. "Home" is where we are right now, where the heart beats.

TATSUKO HOSHINO (1903–1984). One of the best known of the modern Japanese women haiku poets. Hoshino was the second daughter of the famous haiku poet Kyoshi Takahama, who said of her haiku sensibility, "she has a gentle awareness of the shape of nature which she reveals just as it is." She was the leader of the *Tamamo* (Seaweed) haiku group and magazine.

in Buddha believe:
wheat shaft's
green truth

SEISENSUI OGIWARA

Over breakfast I muse about truth, remembering Socrates.
As I look out the window, the two-foot icicles glint in the
sun and my mind stops and only takes in *this*. Perhaps this
is truth, the way things are without overlays of thought and
opinion. It is said we create our own reality, that our percep-
tion of reality is mind's projection. I know that if I had been
depressed or self-absorbed, I would not have seen the icicles,
nor later paid attention to the woman at the store who
needed the door opened. By being present and less preoc-
cupied, the more we see the way things are, as in this haiku:
the green wheat is absolute truth and our interpretation is
relative, subjective truth. The film *Rashomon* is perhaps the

best investigation of "truth" from four people's perspectives of a robbery. Less known is the true story of Won-hyo, the seventh-century Korean monk who traveled to China to seek enlightenment. One night midjourney, he slept in a cave and drank water from a cup in the dark; the next morning he found the cup was actually a human skull. He was revolted yet realized it was his mind's thinking that altered his response, and not the thing itself. The truth of reality was clear to him and he turned back to Korea, becoming a great Buddhist master. Images of him can still be found painted on Korean temples, such as Haein-sa, where I first saw Won-hyo holding the skull as Hamlet did, finding not only the truth of impermanence, but the truth of things as they truly are. A hint of "green truth" that can be found anywhere, even over breakfast.

SEISENSUI OGIWARA (1884–1976). One of the great pioneers of Japanese free-verse haiku. He broke away from the lineages of Kyoshi—and later Hekigodo—to create more subjective haiku. He also formed *Stratus,* the most popular of "free-verse" haiku magazines. He was married but lived as a Buddhist pilgrim for a while. He was also the prolific writer of more than three hundred books: essays, translations from German to Japanese, travel sketches, and haiku.

no sake—
I gaze deeply
at the moon

SANTOKA TANEDA

"Sake for the body; haiku for the heart; sake is the haiku of the body, haiku is the sake of the heart."[45] This is a famous quote by Santoka, "the imperfect monk": a wandering monk of modern times who loved his rice wine as much as haiku and the Buddha. Much of the time he lived in poverty, begging food and drink. So although it is an imperfect evening to enjoy the moon without his beloved sake, he can still sit down with the moon as it—and he—is, with an empty jug beside him, whereas most of us, in contrast, have a harder time accepting imperfections in our own life, for the culture constantly mirrors images of perfection. Most of us lead our lives trying for perfection in a career, house, relationship, or physical appearance. If we could accept things more as they and we are, we would not suffer so much. We need inspiration: Milarepa, the eleventh-century Tibetan poet-yogi, is a great example of imperfection, of someone who went from being a murderer to an enlightened master in one lifetime; in his early life he was a black magician and murdered people to avenge his family, but later regretted his actions and became a student of the Buddhist master Marpa, who put him through terrible trials to awaken him. He finally awakened and spent the rest of his life as a wanderer, chanting realization songs to awaken others; he is always depicted with hand to ear, to hear and sing stories of the "perfection of imperfection."

SANTOKA TANEDA (1882–1940). One of the most famous and eccentric modern Japanese haiku poets. He was rescued from a suicide attempt when young, and went on to become one of the last true Zen pilgrim-monks of the twentieth century. His haiku was as free-style as his life; he used the principle of the haiku spirit, but not the form of any set syllable count or kigo (season word). His haiku in English is found in *Mountain Tasting: Zen Haiku by Santoka Taneda,* translated by John Stevens.

Jasmine

white,

just white,

opening to white space.

JAVIER SOLOGUREN

The white flowers open to it. A bird flies across it. The ballet dancer Nureyev leaps into it, and we awaken to the *space* that makes everything possible, from which everything arises and will return. In some cultures there are aesthetic terms relating to space. In China there is feng shui, the art of divination, creating an auspicious, harmonious placement of things within the space. In Japan, there is *ma*, the artistic balance of the physical and psychological space existing between people and things, found in the traditional arts known for their sparseness. In painting, the dominant white space swallows the black ink strokes of a few blades of grass. In architecture the open space is more important than the things within the space, for if the room is cluttered, we cannot see the jasmine in the white room, large or small. Perhaps in this haiku the jasmine is unfolding under the open sky. This empty space affects us: it pulls us in, inviting us to connect our mind to it. In Tibetan Buddhist texts, our natural, relaxed state of mind is said to be like space. The Vajra Regent Ösel Tendzin explained this view of meditation, "According to the Kagyu gurus, space is the true nature of mind . . . empty and luminous at the same time . . . a mind whose reference point is free from grasping and fixation is like space. . . . The technique is to dissolve the conceptual mind into the breath, which dissolves into space."[46] This state of openness to our world is available when there is a gap in our confusion and torrent of thoughts; what is left in that moment is space. Then our mind becomes like the space in which flowers open just so, like jasmine.

JAVIER SOLOGUREN (1921–2004). Well-known poet and prolific translator in his native country Peru. Sologuren translated from Spanish, French, Italian, Swedish, and Japanese. He lived in Japan for a while and translated much literature, and thus experimented with haiku. Mostly a free-verse poet; his main poetry collection is *Vida Contina* (A Continuous Life).

> dusting off
> his father's sheet music—
> spring moon

> KRIS MOON KONDO

Music and song, the primal urge to express delight in the world, to breathe energy into the world. We sing to express our aliveness: alone in the shower, a group in a Dublin pub, a Pavaroti on stage, or native people around a fire. On key or off, it doesn't matter; whether a Mozart cantata or the guitar blues, we sing because we are alive. I remember my father telling me of the old "bicycle trains" in Illinois, where his club, *The Sprockets*, would meet in the rail yard, put their bikes in one train car and sit in another, singing 1940s songs together for hours, all the way to the countryside, where they would ride their bikes, energized by their singing. In postmodern culture, because we mostly listen to others singing with our private earplugs rather than singing ourselves, we have lost this active participation in everyday life. We could use stronger spontaneous energy, the masculine energy that exists within everything and everyone, male or female. In Tibetan Buddhism it called "the masculine principle," which is (in balance with the feminine principle of wisdom and space) "the energy of skillful means," the warm dynamic energy to act. To do what needs to be done: to nurse what needs to be nursed and destroy what needs to be destroyed. A time to tell the child a story and a time to discipline the child. A time to sing and a time to be silent. Yet the energy bank is always there to tap into and express, as in this haiku, where perhaps a son or daughter pauses, remembering the father's family, and carrying on the energy of his lineage under the new moon.

KRIS MOON KONDO (b. 1946). A well-known active haiku poet who also writes renku (group linked verse). In 1989, along with Tadashi Kondo, she formed AIR (Association for International Renku). Having lived most of her adult life in Japan, she actively participates in and leads poetry groups in Japan and America, publishes widely in magazines, and gives art exhibitions of her *haiga* (haiku with a painting). Her haiku collection is *Through a Window*.

Summer night:
in my eyes starlight
hundreds of years old

GEORGE SWEDE

Another suicide bomber in the news. The feeling of power-
lessness and marginalization of so many people worldwide,
resorting to extreme methods such as martyrdom to feel
their power again. The tough balance of power in this world.
Worldly or outer power through money, talent, beauty, con-
nections; or through stealing, corruption, suppression, and
murder. We all want to feel powerful, to have something em-
powering in our life. Yet the only true power is innate power,
like sap running through trees, power that we all have from
birth. No matter who we are, rich or poor, we can feel this
inner power even momentarily, like the poet in this haiku
realizing that we are part of a vaster reality, that we have the

power of ancient stars in our eyes. In Tibet this is called *drala,* cosmic force energy that we can tap into anytime, anywhere. The "spirituals and the blues" are an example of drala, as songs that America's black culture used during slavery and the civil rights movement especially to empower themselves, to remind themselves of their true transcendent humanity as beings of the universe, beyond their suffering. Yet sometimes the powerless need help to feel their innate power; those of us empowered can help and empower others, remind others of their inner resources. The real work of this life seems to be to alleviate the suffering of others, so they can feel their power again, if only by our looking at the stars together for a moment from this tough planet.

GEORGE SWEDE (b. 1940). One of the foremost Canadian haiku poets, originally from Latvia. He is also a professor, physician, and a promoter of haiku. He published and edited the *Canadian Haiku Anthology* in 1979. His works include *Wingbeats, Eye to Eye with a Frog,* and *My Shadow Doing Something.*

> for everyday clothes
> an everyday mind—
> peach blossoms

AYAKO HOSOMI

"Peach blossoms" would be an admirable answer to the Zen *koan* (teaching question), "What is ultimate reality?" A famous traditional answer is "the cypress tree in the garden." It is so "everyday," just like when we wear old clothes to do chores—doing dishes, mopping floors, cleaning toilets, washing clothes—make up much of our everyday life. And since, worldwide, chores are still more of a woman's reality than a man's, it is not surprising that this haiku was written by a woman—and it's one of her most famous haiku. And because the poet does not make a distinction between the everyday and admiring the blossoms, she is expressing the "true ordinary mind" spoken of in wisdom traditions. The everyday world and the blossoms are equal parts of our sacred world. In this way, instead of being drudgery, our chores become an everyday awareness practice. By putting our mind on the weight of the dish, the smoothness of the porcelain, and the water through our fingers, by totally focusing on this one thing only, other thoughts drop away and we become relaxed with our everyday mind, in our everyday clothes.

AYAKO HOSOMI (1907–1997). One of the more outstanding Japanese women haiku poets of the modern era. She participated in the haiku group Kaze (Wind) that her husband, haiku poet Kinichi Sawaki, was a part of. Her ten collections include *Furubaru* (Winter Rose) and *Momo wa Yae* (Eight-Petaled Peach Flowers).

winds of autumn—
water less transparent
than the fins of a fish

TAKAJO MITSUHASHI

There are three habitual styles of approaching the world:
through passion, through aggression, and through ignorance.
That is, we pull things to us, push things away from us, or ig-
nore things. Although each style causes suffering, each style
has its enlightened side of compassion, nonaggression, and
clear seeing. However, ignorance is the most deceptive, for
it is the least transparent and seems quite harmless, this not
wanting to see things as they are, for things are sometimes too
painful, too embarrassing, too overwhelming. Yet the conse-
quence of ignorance is gravest suffering, such as the genocide
of the Cambodian killing fields, and is something to reflect
upon as in this famed quote by Edmund Burke, "The only

thing necessary for the triumph of evil is for good men to do nothing." Yet what makes the darkest of times the best of times is that in difficult times our tendency to ignore doesn't work anymore, for the terrible has become too transparent to ignore. So we are awakened and must act. As hinted at in this haiku, if we were in an ignorant mode, we would not be able to notice that the fins of the fish are actually clearer than the water, or at least seem to be, depending on the quality of the water; it is something we wouldn't normally take notice of. However, this simple practice of transforming ignorance step by step, by noticing the small things around us, could just possibly at some point tip the ignorance quota of the world into clear wisdom, where all is transparent.

TAKAJO MITSUHASHI (1899–1972). One of the great modern Japanese women haiku poets, one of the four *T*'s. She first wrote traditional haiku under the tutelage of her husband, but then turned to experimental haiku along with other women poets. Her poetry can be found in *Shida Jigoku* (The Fern Hell). Her suffering during World War II produced *Hakkotsu* (The Bleached Bones). Though in poor health the last ten years of her life, she kept writing haiku. This one is from an early collection, *Uo no Hire* (Fins of a Fish).

Your shadow
on the page
the poem.

CID CORMAN

It is uncanny that we have to constantly remind ourselves
that there is only *now,* this very moment. So many books and
wisdom traditions speak of this power of the now. We are so
caught up in hope and fear about the future or rethinking the
past, that we are rarely in this present moment. Caught up in
our mind's running from one scene and dialogue to another,
we are actors, more like the figures in a Balinese shadow pup-
pet play. Even stopping while reading this very page can bring
us back: take in a few breaths right now, breathing deeply . . .
It is that simple, but not that simple to make it a constant
habit, of bringing our attention back, again and again and
again. But the stakes are high: the sanity and relaxation of

our own mind, the ability to really see what is around us, and a deeper appreciation of our life. Corman's haiku brings us back with its deceptive simplicity, like a delicate shock to the anonymous center of it all. He says of poetry, "It is not a matter of meaning, but of livingdying."[47] With all the poignancy that the dream shadow of impermanence and death brings, in between we have the poem, which is just this brief moment of our being with "our shadow" on this very page.

CID CORMAN (1924–2004). American poet, translator, and editor of the seminal magazine *Origin*. He lived as an expatriate, first in Europe but mostly in Kyoto, Japan. He's best known for the co-translation, with Kamaike Susumu, of Basho's travel journal, *Back Roads to Far Towns*. His works include *Livingdying* and *The Famous Blue Aerogrammes*. Known for his minimalist style, using every word as if it were a pristine grain of sand, he used haiku to express philosophical simplicity.

shall we die together,
my lover whispers—
evening fireflies

MASAJO SUZUKI

The power of love. It is the deepest human emotion we experience in our lifetime. Masajo Suzuki's haiku epitomizes the idealized great romantic passion, for her objective imagery is dyed in her feelings, as if writing on white paper soaked in hues of red. This love haiku was amazingly written when she was eighty-eight years old; and even at ninety-five, I witnessed her still talking passionately about recent visions of her lover. This passion makes us feel intensely, do crazy neurotic things, and go beyond ourselves. Sappho expressed it also for all time in her poem-fragment: "Suddenly, as a whirlwind against an oak tree, love shakes my heart."[48] At these peak dramatic moments, most of us want to solidify it

199

forever, and some even fantasize suicide. However, this approach to love is what Trungpa Rinpoche called ego-fixation: "We are blinded by our clinging. The object of passion, instead of being bathed in the intense warmth of free passion, feels oppressed by our stifling heat of neurotic passion. Free passion is radiation without a radiator."[49] Yet this tantric teacher and passionate lover advocated neither negating nor indulging this intense passion, but rather working with it to transmute it into open radiating love. If we could follow this path, then love would not just burn brightly and go out quickly like a firefly, but also transform us into another level of being, as nothing else in the world can do. Nothing but naked love, with no self and no lover. Nothing left but pure passion and pure love, burning: "roses of fire."

MASAJO SUZUKI (1906–2003). One of the most infamous, passionate modern Japanese women haiku poets who wrote love poems in the haiku form. Having a love affair while married, and writing about it as well, was unusual for a woman of her day. She also lived a passionate life with her close circle of poets around the pub-restaurant she ran in Tokyo. English selections from her works can be found in *Love Haiku: Masajo Suzuki's Lifetime of Love,* translated by Lee Gurga and Emiko Miyashita with an introduction by Patricia Donegan and Yoshie Ishibashi.

in the dark
where you undress
a blooming iris

NOBUKO KATSURA

I trace the nude bodies in white marble with my eyes, and
then trace them with my fingertips: a child of ten, mesmer-
ized, looking at the photograph of Auguste Rodin's carved
statue, *The Kiss*. Years later I touch a real lover in the flesh and
enter more deeply into the realm of the erotic. This memory
of sensual touch haunts us always, whether a fleeting image,
a brief touch with a stranger, nights of long lovemaking with
a devoted lover, or years of sleeping close with the familiar
one; it doesn't matter. What matters is that we were touched
in some way, sometime, somewhere, and, once touched by
love, by the erotic, it is never forgotten, no matter how small
or how great. We know our body was touched, our mind was

touched, the touch triggering thoughts and feelings inseparable from touch; for the lover's own body and mind are *one*. And perhaps unknown to the one touching or being touched, we enter a primordial, sacred state. We are transformed as we enter the place of openness and connection, no matter how fleeting—a transformation celebrated in love songs and erotic art throughout history; a transformation celebrated by Walt Whitman: "I sing the body electric . . ."[50] And diarist Anaïs Nin: "It is not merely a heightened sensual fusion . . . but an ecstatic awareness of the whole of life."[51] Yet sometimes the lover's mind is selfish and sometimes closed, but amid the touching there is always an open crack, a state of grace, an altered state of being that occurs. It is this unveiled, naked state of being that we eternally seek, as epitomized in this haiku's sensual imagery: the iris petals perpetually opening and opening and opening.

NOBUKO KATSURA (1914–2004). A prominent Japanese woman haiku poet of the modern era and protégé of the haiku poet Sojo Hino. After World War II and the loss of her husband, she worked as a secretary while editing the magazine *Josei Haiku* (Women's Haiku) with Chiyoko Kato. She also founded the magazine *Soen* (Grass Garden). In 1992 she received one of the most prestigious haiku awards, the Dakotsu Prize. Her works include *Gekko Sho* (Beams of the Moon), *Nyoshin* (The Female Body), and *Kaei* (Shadows of Flowers).

the vast night—
now nothing left
but the fragrance

JORGE LUIS BORGES

The power of memory is especially related to our senses, and especially to scent—the most primordial of the five senses. One recalls the famous passage of Marcel Proust's flood of memories streaming from the smell and taste of one madeleine cookie in his novel *Swann's Way*. One can more easily recall the triggers of one's own deep memory-bank. A trigger perhaps of wood smoke, oranges, or rain … bringing up good, bad, happy, or sad memories, depending. How the realm of memory, dream, and the unconscious are all so very intertwined. How memory is evocative, more like the fluidity of Virginia Woolf's poetic play of light in and out of the waves of the sea in her novel *The Waves*. How it is essential to remember that memories trigger both truths and untruths, the real and the unreal—and memory cannot always discern the difference. Yet it seems so real in this moment of time, for memory is an old trickster. The dark vast night now a memory and, although faint, something remains in the scent we still appreciate: perhaps the scent of perfume, flowers, wine, or skin . . . Borges touching the stream of consciousness brings all of these worlds together in one breath of words, in one breath of lingering fragrance.

JORGE LUIS BORGES (1899–1986). Famed Argentine short-story writer, essayist, and poet. His early years were devoted to poetry and later to essays on metaphysics and literature. Due to poor health and eyesight, he turned to short fiction, which was known for its fantasy and esoteric style. Among his works are *Luna de enfrente* (poetry), *El Aleph* (fiction), and *Inquisiciones* (essays); an English compilation of stories and essays are presented in *Labyrinths.* He also dabbled in haiku and other poetic forms.

Derelict with eyes
I settle in a quiet
Carnival of waves.

SONIA SANCHEZ

The eyes of the poor and disenfranchised, those usually ignored. The eyes look out at us and we look into them—that is, if we dare to look. We can if we recognize that innate inner richness is the most amazing thing about being a human being, no matter who we are, as Ruby Dee, the African-American actress and activist, proclaims. And in this haiku, the "quiet carnival of waves" points to that spark of aliveness existing within every person. A visionary such as Nobel laureate Muhammad Yunus of Bangladesh is using inner richness as the base for his practical concept of empowering the poor to empower themselves. This is done by "microcredit": giving small loans to poor people, including beggars, to help them out of poverty.[52] His vision is to eliminate global poverty by 2050. For this to occur, a new social consciousness has to include a caring belief in the unlimited potential of *all* human beings, if given an opportunity. On this level, any of us with only a little money ($15.00 on average) can give a loan via the Internet to those with no money. This in turn brings out the inner richness of us all. For the waves of connection really only exist from person to person, from eye to eye. The Koreans call this eye-communication *nun-kil* or "eye-street": that pathway or pathwave of connection existing between two people. It only has to be recognized so it can reverberate, with eyes quietly reveling together.

SONIA SANCHEZ (b. 1934). A well-known African-American poet, playwright, political activist, and scholar. Among her many poetry collections are *Does Your House Have Lions, Like the Singing Coming Off the Drum, Shake Loose My Skin,* and *Homegirls and Handgrenades,* which won an American Book Award. She reclaims the territory of poetry's base in music and song, especially with jazz, even with her experimentation with haiku.

the war—

yet

these little birds

YVES GERBAL

There is not one wisdom tradition that says that peace comes out of war. All speak to peace coming from peaceful means. Thinking of world peace is overwhelming, yet it seems more possible if we can think of working on a smaller, individual scale, something we can directly work with: ourselves. The Dalai Lama sums it up: "Without inner peace, it is not possible to have world peace."[53] So the challenge for each of us is to find some method—be it meditation, prayer, slowing down, or self-reflection—to bring us back to our softer innate nature, existing behind the hardened shell of inner confusion and turmoil. However, the goal is not to always feel nice and peaceful but to be with our experience and feelings just as they are; and in turn, this simple let-it-be approach gives rise to a sense of well-being. And being kinder, more embracing to our own inner turmoil makes us feel more at ease and kinder to others as well. Perhaps both aggression and compassion are built into our DNA chromosomes, yet one thing is certain: if we can see the war raging around us as a reflection of the war raging within us, it can be a deep awakening for us to soften further. Coming back to the present moment of seeing the fragile little birds peeping, as in this haiku, automatically softens us even in the midst of war. Even a momentary lessening of our own inner turmoil gives us a gap, a glimmer of inner peace, and this tiny expression of gentleness plants seeds of peace within us and around us. The birds remind us, and lead us in heralding the dawn.

YVES GERBAL (b. 1959). Well-known and active modern haiku poet in France. Some of his work appears in *Anthologie du HAIKU en France*, translated by Agostini, Cannarozzi, Morgan, Py, et al.

"air raids night after night"

clear stars
in the cold night
after the planes' roar

HIDENO ISHIBASHI

The horror and poignancy of war's universal experience are expressed through a woman's eyes in this haiku. Usually we get the experience of war through a male perspective, but there are some courageous women writers, such as Hideno Ishibashi, who lived through the bombings of Tokyo during World War II and simply documented her experience through haiku. It is only recently that non-Japanese are finally becoming aware of the war atrocities of more civilians being killed in the Tokyo and other cities' bombings than in the combined atomic bombings of Hiroshima and Nagasaki. Here in the midst of air raids, we get the human dimension: the resilient capacity of the human spirit under

209

dire circumstances to be able to appreciate the crystal clear stars on a freezing night, in the stillness after the roar of the planes diminishes . . . Then it is just the silent stars overhead and the eyes of a woman staring up into vast space, in awe of this almost terrible beauty that remains after the human destruction. Just clear stars and the sound of our own heartbeats: the sacred remains.

HIDENO ISHIBASHI (1909–1947). An outstanding Japanese woman haiku poet of modern times. From her youth she had famous teachers, including the haiku poet Kyoshi and the tanka poet Akiko Yosano. She later had haiku meetings with Riichi Yokomitsu. She was married to the renowned haiku critic Kenkichi Yamamoto (1907–1988), and they had one daughter. Hideno died in Kyoto from tuberculosis and war trauma. Her one collection, *Sakura Koku* (Cherry Blossoms Deep), won the prestigious Kawabata Bosha Prize. Translations of her haiku can be found in *Far from the Field: Haiku by Japanese Women,* translated and edited by Makoto Ueda.

"compassion instead of revenge"

to the one breaking it—
the fragrance
of the plum

CHIYO-NI

Her clothes burned off, the naked Vietnamese girl is running, running down the road, running for her life; red-hot napalm firebombs trail after her. She is screaming, crying out in agony with arms outstretched, as if signaling, signaling to us for help . . . That was the unforgettable image of 1972, the Pulizer-prize–winning photo of the nine-year-old girl that personalized the horror of the war for us in America and worldwide, and helped end it. Thirty years later, I hear a lecture by this now-grown woman, Kim Phuc, who not only amazingly survived that experience, but who has forgiven her attackers and is now circling the globe, working for UNESCO and her own foundation for war-torn children, telling her story as a "goodwill ambassador," arms outstretched for peace. In this haiku's depiction, although a hand breaks the branch of the flowering plum to enjoy its scent and beauty—the tree, like the Vietnamese woman, reaches out and gives back its deepest fragrance. This is what Christians call the act of "forgiving one's enemies," which is beyond any human logic or comprehension. Yet in the end, it may be the only thing that works, that will bring us lasting peace: to reach out to the other, to finally heal what has been broken, this cracking of a plum branch.

CHIYO-NI (1703–1775), or Kaga no Chiyo; her family name was Fukumasuya. One of the greatest traditional Japanese women haiku poets. Born into a scroll maker's family, she studied with two of Basho's disciples, was a renowned renga master, painter, and Buddhist nun. She published two poetry books: *Chiyo-ni Kushu* (Chiyo-ni's Haiku Collection) and *Matsu no Koe* (Voice of the Pine). Known for living Basho's "Way of Haiku." See *Chiyo-ni: Woman Haiku Master* by Patricia Donegan and Yoshie Ishibashi.

in between
the Kabul bombings—
voices of crickets

PATRICIA DONEGAN

I've always been attuned to crickets, almost living for their sound. The sound primordial as a heartbeat, as seeds swelling under the earth, as deep breaths, the sound reassuring to keep us going in the darkest of nights. That night of October 11, 2001, I heard the crickets again, not only from my Tokyo window, but from my TV. Watching the live newscast of the American bombing in Afghanistan, I could hear the crickets chirping in Kabul in between the flashing; it was so loud that the newsman also noted it. In the incessant sound of Nature's crickets, beyond the U.S. bombing of Kabul, beyond the devastation of the Bamiyan Buddhas, beyond the countless suicide bombings, there is the eternal space in which we all can pause, in which we can hear the crickets. For each and every moment is a chance for us personally, to choose either aggression or non-aggression, to choose not to be a part of the destructive cycle of violence begetting violence. For as the ancient Buddhist text the *Dhammapada* says: "Hatred never ceases by hatred; but by love alone is healed. This is an ancient and eternal law." We can see this ancient law at work in the power of non-aggression manifested in the actions and life of Mahatma Gandhi, the promoter of *satyagraha* (nonviolent resistance). We can follow this eternal law by expanding our own vision and working toward eliminating aggression on all levels: mental, verbal, personal, and social. And we can know that even in the small act of pausing to hear the crickets, we are also pausing for peace.

PATRICIA DONEGAN (b. 1945). American poet, translator, and promoter of haiku as an awareness practice. She was faculty of East-West poetics at Naropa University under Allen Ginsberg and Chögyam Trungpa, a student of haiku master Seishi Yamaguchi, and a Fulbright scholar to Japan. She is a meditation teacher and the poetry editor of *Kyoto Journal.* Her haiku works include *Chiyo-ni: Woman Haiku Master,* co-translated with Yoshie Ishibashi, and *Haiku: Asian Arts and Crafts for Creative Kids.* Her poetry collections include *Without Warning, Hot Haiku, Heralding the Milk Light,* and a haiku selection in the anthology *The Unswept Path.*

raging seas—
lying over Sado island
the Milky Way

BASHO MATSUO

We are caught in this human realm; caught in the eternal cosmic dance of creation and destruction; caught in the symbolic dance of the ancient Hindu god Shiva dancing within a circle of fire energy. We are caught in the dark, in the "raging seas" of our earthy island's smashed skulls, slashed throats, and tortured minds—and we are also caught in its light: in the awakening songs of the morning birds outside our window, heralding the light of our sun among millions in our Milky Way. Here the haiku pinpoints this poignancy of being caught, for in Basho's time Sado Island was a prison preserve for the exiled. As for all of us, there is no escaping the dance we are born into. We can only trust the dance that is happening within the teardrop of it all . . . that is the teardrop of compassion within us. Our only refuge is to embrace the still point of the dancing, of no birth and no death, of no heaven and no hell. To step beyond the cynicism of our postmodern world. To step beyond hope and fear, and trust the still point: the pregnant moment of now, of always becoming. This is the refuge of peace within us and outside of us: to keep the still point of the dance. As in the Navajo chant-blessing[54] I paraphrased: In beauty may we walk, beauty before us, behind us, above us, below us, with beauty all around us may we walk. May we walk in this circle of beauty and know that it is *one:* the trail of tears and laughter; the trail of war and peace. May we always walk in the energy of light, the light of the Milky Way. May we walk in this moment's beauty. May we continue to dance. It is finished in beauty. It is finished in beauty. It is finished in beauty.

BASHO MATSUO (1644–1694). The greatest haiku poet in Japanese history. Coming from a low samurai class, he later became a renga master with many disciples, studied Zen, and traveled widely. He took haiku to a deeper level, espousing haikai no michi (the Way of Haiku) as a way of life and a return to Nature. See *Sarumino* (*Monkey's Raincoat,* a renga collection); and *Oku no Hosomichi* (*Narrow Road to the Interior,* a haibun collection). See also haiku translations in R. H. Blyth's *History of Haiku,* vol. 1 and Makoto Ueda's translation *Basho and His Interpreters*—just some among many translations.

NOTES

1. Taizan Maezumi Roshi, *The Way of Everyday Life: Zen Master Dogen's Genjokoan*, with commentary by Maezumi (Los Angeles: Zen Center of L.A. Zen Writing Series, 1978) from "Commentary Four."

2. Asataro Miyamori, *An Anthology of Haiku, Ancient and Modern* (Tokyo: Maruzen, 1932), 439.

3. Yoshinobu Hakutani and Robert L. Tener, eds., *Haiku: The Other World by Richard Wright* (New York: Arcade Publishing, 1998), x.

4. Chögyam Trungpa Rinpoche, *The Sadhana of Mahamudra: Which Quells the Mighty Warring of the Three Lords of Materialism and Brings Realization of the Ocean of Siddis of the Practice Lineage* (Halifax: Nalanda Translation Committee, 1968), 19.

5. Sakyong Mipham Rinpoche, *Ruling Your World* (New York: Morgan Road Books, 2005), 160–63.

6. Kazuaki Tanahashi and Roko Sherry Chayat, *Endless Vow: The Zen Path of Soen Nakagawa* (Boston: Shambhala Publications, 1996), 101–2.

7. Daisetz T. Suzuki, "Prajna Paramita Heart Sutra: Daily Zen

Sutras" in *The Manual of Zen Buddhism* (New York: Grove Press, 1960), 26.

8. Justin Wintle, *History of Islam* (London: Rough Guides Ltd., 2003), 86.

9. Huston Smith, *Islam: A Concise Introduction* (San Francisco: HarperCollins Books, 2001), 82.

10. Donald Richie, interview by Yoshie Ishibashi Osawa, "The View to Mt. Sumeru: Donald Richie on D. T. Suzuki" in *Kyoto Journal* 65 (2007): 20–23.

11. Frederic Brussat and Mary Ann Brussat, *Spiritual Literacy: Reading the Sacred in Everyday Life* (New York: Simon & Schuster, 1996), 244.

12. Dylan Thomas, "Do Not Go Gently into That Good Night" in Oscar Williams, ed., *The Pocket Book of Modern Verse* (New York: Washington Square Press, 1961), 574.

13. Cynthia Kneen, *Awake Mind, Open Heart: The Power of Courage and Dignity in Everyday* Life (New York: Marlowe and Company, 2002), 129, 131.

14. Thich Nhat Hanh, *Present Moment Wonderful Moment: Mindfulness Verses in Daily Living* (Berkeley: Parallax Press, 1990), 65.

15. Antoine de Saint Exupery, *The Little Prince*, trans. Katherine Woods (New York: Harcourt Brace Javanovich, 1943, 1971), 70.

16. Makoto Ueda, "Basho on the Art of the Haiku" in *Literary and Art Theories in Japan* (Cleveland: The Press of Western Reserve University, 1967), 159.

17. Paul Reps, ed., "Buddha Twirls a Flower" in *Zen Flesh, Zen Bones:*

A *Collection of Zen and Pre-Zen Writings* (New York: Doubleday & Co., 1975), 95.

18. "Unless you become like a child, you cannot enter the kingdom of heaven." Matthew 18:3.

19. "For now we see through a glass darkly; but then face to face." I Corinthians 13:11.

20. Brussat and Brussat, *Spiritual Literacy,* 409.

21. T. C. McLuhan, *Touch the Earth: A Self Portrait of Indian Existence* (New York: Simon & Schuster, 1971), 107.

22. Kabir Helminski, ed. and trans., *The Pocket Rumi Reader* (Boston: Shambhala Publications, 2001), 80.

23. Daisetz T. Suzuki, "Zen and Haiku" in *Zen and Japanese Culture* (New York: Princeton University Press, 1959), 245–46.

24. Pema Chödrön, *When Things Fall Apart: Heart Advice for Difficult Times* (Boston: Shambhala Publications, 1997), 115.

25. Kenneth Cragg, ed. and trans., *Readings in the Qur'an* (New York: HarperCollins, 1988).

26. Percy Bysshe Shelley, "Ode to the West Wind" in Oscar Williams, ed., *Immortal Poems of the English Language* (New York: Washington Square Press, 1964), 297–99.

27. Violet (Matusuda) de Christoforo, *May Sky—There's Always Tomorrow: A History and Anthology of Haiku* (Los Angeles: Sun and Moon Press, 1996).

28. Kent Nerburn and Louise Menglekoch, eds., *Native American Wisdom* (Novato, Calif.: New World Library, 1991), 1–2.

29. Patricia Donegan, "Haiku and the Ecotastrophe" in Allan

Badiner, ed., *Dharma Gaia: A Harvest of Essays in Buddhism and Ecology* (Berkeley: Parallax Press, 1990), 205.

30. Masaru Emoto, *The Hidden Messages in Water* (Hillsboro, Ore.: Beyond Words Publishing, 2004).

31. Gary Snyder, "The Etiquette of Freedom" in *The Practice of the Wild: Essays by Gary Snyder* (San Francisco: North Point Press, 1990), 6.

32. Oseko Toshiharu, *Basho's Haiku: Literal Translations for Those Who Wish to Read the Original Japanese* (Tokyo: Maruzen Co., Ltd., 1990), 4a (2).

33. Wing-tsit Chan, trans., *The Way of Lao-tzu* (Indianapolis: Bobbs-Merill, 1963).

34. Stephen Mitchell, *The Enlightened Mind: An Anthology of Sacred Prose* (New York: HarperCollins, 1991), 114.

35. Susan Edwards, *Blistering Fossils* (unpublished poems).

36. Ko Un, interview by Patricia Donegan, "Ko Un: Human Nature Itself Is Poetic" in *Kyoto Journal* 60 (2005): 36.

37. Chögyam Trungpa Rinpoche, *Shambhala: Sacred Path of the Warrior* (Boston: Shambhala Publications, 1984), 28.

38. William Blake, "Auguries of Innocence" in Oscar William, ed., *Immortal Poems of the English Language* (New York: Washington Square Press, 1964), 227.

39. Joseph Campbell, "Masks of Eternity" in Betty S. Flowers, ed., *The Power of Myth: With Bill Moyers* (New York: Doubleday, 1988), 229.

40. John Brandi and Dennis Maloney, eds., *The Unswept Path:*

Contemporary American Haiku (New York: White Pine Press, 2005), 72.

41. Robert Aitken, *The Morning Star: New and Selected Zen Writings* (Washington, D.C.: Shoemaker & Hoard Publishers, 2003), 219–22.

42. Clayborne Carson, ed., *The Autobiography of Martin Luther King, Jr.* (New York: Warner Books, 1998), 189.

43. Chögyam Trungpa Rinpoche, "The Lion's Roar" in *The Myth of Freedom: And the Way of Meditation* (Berkeley: Shambhala Publications, 1976), 69.

44. Tadashi Kondo, interview by Patricia Donegan, "Poetry for Peace: The United Nations of Renku" in *Kyoto Journal* 52 (2003): 43.

45. John Stevens, introduction to *Mountain Tasting: Zen Haiku by Santoka Taneda* (Tokyo: Weatherhill, 1980), 24.

46. Vajra Regent Ösel Tendzin, *Space, Time and Energy* (Ojai, Calif.: Satdharma Press, 2000), 14–18.

47. Brandi and Maloney, *The Unswept Path*, 62.

48. This is my own English translated version; many book translations are available: for example, Mary Bernard, fragment 44 in *Sappho: A New Translation* (Berkeley: University of California Press, 1958).

49. Trungpa, *The Myth of Freedom*, 87.

50. Walt Whitman, "I Sing the Body Electric" in John Kouwenhoven, ed., *Leaves of Grass and Selected Prose by Walt Whitman* (New York: The Modern Library, 1950), 78.

51. Braussat and Brussat, *Spiritual Literacy*, 531.

52. Muhammed Yunas, interview by Charlie Rose, *The Charlie Rose Show*, PBS, January 10, 2008.

53. Dalai Lama, *His Holiness the Dalai Lama: In My Own Words*, ed. Mary Craig (London: Hodder & Stoughton, 2001), 112.

54. Grove Day, *The Sky Clears: Poetry of the American Indians* (New York: Macmillan, 1951), 64, 75.

CREDITS

Grateful acknowledgement is made for permission to reprint the following copyrighted material:

Aitken, Robert: "The sun glitters" from *The Morning Star,* Shoemaker & Hoard Publishers, copyright © 2003 by Honolulu Diamond Sangha. Reprinted by permission of the author. Amann, Eric: "shorter kisses" from *Haiku World* edited by William J. Higginson, Kodansha International, copyright © 1996 by Eric Amann. Reprinted by permission of the author. Brandi, John: "after the rain" from *The Unswept Path* edited by John Brandi and Dennis Maloney, White Pine Press (www.whitepine.org), copyright © 2005 by John Brandi. Reprinted by permission of the author. Cain, Jack: "the wind" from *Four Seasons* edited by Koko Kato, Ko Poetry Association, copyright © 1991 by Jack Cain. Reprinted by permission of the author. Cain, Jack: "an empty elevator" from *The Haiku Anthology* edited by Cor van den Heuvel, W. W. Norton & Co., copyright © 1991 by Jack Cain. Reprinted by permission of the author. Chula, Margaret: "remembering those gone" from *The Smell of Rust,* Katsura Press, copyright © 2003 by Margaret Chula. Reprinted by permission of the author. Cobb, David: "across the fields of stubble" from *Mounting Shadows*, Equinox Press, copyright © 1992 by David Cobb. Reprinted by permission of the author. Codrescu, Ion: "when the spade turns" from *Unsold Flowers*, Hub Editions, copyright © 1995 by Ion Codrescu. Reprinted by permission of the author. Corman, Cid: "Your shadow" from *The Unswept Path* edited by John Brandi and Dennis Maloney, White Pine Press (www.whitepine.org), copyright © 2005 by Cid Corman. Reprinted by permission of White Pine Press. Davidson, L. A.: "winter morning" from *The Shape of the Tree* by Wind Chimes Roth and Glen Burnie, DLT Association, copyright © 1982 L. A. Davidson. Reprinted by permission of Laura Tanna. Deming, Kristen: "migrating birds" from *Eyes of the Blossoms*, copyright © 1997 by Kristen Deming. Reprinted by permission of the author. di Prima, Diane: "the inner tide" from *The Unswept Path* edited by John Brandi and Dennis Maloney, White Pine Press (www.whitepine.org), copyright © 2005 by Diane di Prima. Reprinted by permission of the author. All rights reserved. Donegan, Patricia: "in between" from *The Unswept Path* edited by John Brandi and Dennis Maloney, White Pine Press (www.whitepine.org), copyright © 2005 by Patricia Donegan. Reprinted by permission of the author. Edwards, Susan: "the moon," copyright © 2008 by Susan Edwards. Reprinted by permission of the author. Gay, Garry: "reflected" from *Haiku* edited by Jackie Hardy, Tuttle Publishing, copyright © 2002 by Garry Gay. Reprinted by permission of the author. Ginsberg, Allen: "to see void, vast infinite . . . blue sky" from page 81 of *Death & Fame: Last Poems 1993–1997* by Allen Gins-

INDEX OF POETS